Contents

Introduction

This book is a guide to the principles of modelling with fabric for the aspiring designer. It provides a systematic course of instruction which covers the modelling of blocks (basic patterns) and their development into garment designs, followed by the modelling of clothes for special occasions. The book is arranged with the simpler exercises at the beginning and the more complex at the end.

Modelling on the dress stand is an essential part of any designer's training. However the original patterns may be acquired – by modelling, flat pattern cutting, drafting or straight from the computer – the final evaluation on the dress stand demands the critical eye and manipulative skills of a designer who understands fabric and fit, how the design should look on the body when still or in movement and if the design is right for that fabric. Such skills are developed through working on the stand.

The book is intended for students and teachers involved in dress design in schools and in fashion and art colleges on courses up to and including degree level; for practitioners in design and sample rooms in the clothing industry; and for individual designer dressmakers needing to make informed judgements before and during the process of transforming fabric into garments. Any dressmaker wishing to gain a greater understanding of the relationship between garment and wearer will find this by using the dress stand throughout a project: the stand is not just something on which to display the finished garment. The first step in learning to design clothes is to understand the three-dimensional shape of the human form and to appreciate the possibilities and the limitations of manipulating flat fabric to the body's contours.

The first part of the book deals with achieving the correct shape and size on the dress stand through understanding the difference between the stand's measurements and the tolerance which must be added to allow for normal body movement when wearing clothes. The measurement charts indicate the amount of tolerance to be added.

This is followed by the modelling of basic blocks to classic lines, a valuable grounding in practising the techniques used in design rooms which appear almost magical to the uninitiated. The blocks can be used as a reference library and be copied without the need to re-model similar designs, a great saving of time and energy in a busy design studio or designer/dressmaker enterprise. Block development simply means learning to adapt the blocks to various styles: different necklines, sleeves and skirt shapes and added openings.

the Stand

I would like to express my thanks to a few special people who have believed in my concept of an 'easy speak' or more visual approach to presenting a book on the subject of modelling on the stand. To Professor Dianne Taylor, Savannah College of Art and Design, Savannah, Georgia, USA (former Dean, School of Fashion Design and Technology, London College of Fashion) for her strong support and continued interest. To the staff of the D.A.L.I. (Developments at London Institute) Professional Development Unit, London College of Fashion, whose enthusiasm and support for my teaching methods has led to something of a revival in the demand for classes on this subject. To Alex Roll, former Course Director, for first giving me the opportunity to develop modelling as an exciting and challenging subject for aspiring fashion designers. To Jan Miller, D.A.L.I. Business Manager, Alanah Cullen, Course Director and Catherine Fuller, for their continued support and interest. To Kennett and Lindsell, for the generous loan of the dress stand featured in the diagrams.

My grateful thanks are also due to my husband for his invaluable advice, encouragement and critical eye; and to my editors, Richard Reynolds and Martina Stansbie of B.T. Batsford Ltd for their guidance and advice on drawings and text.

Fisrt published 1996
Reprinted 2001

Printed and bound in Spain by Bookprint, S.L, Barcelona

B.T. Batsford Ltd
9 Blenheim Court
Brewery Road
London N7 9NT

A member of the Chrysalis Group plc

A CIP catalogue record for this book is available from the British Library

ISBN 0 7134 7757 1

Front cover photography by Ben Jennings

One of the main aims of the book is to remove the mystique surrounding this subject and to demonstrate how, having developed the basic skills, the reader can quickly progress to interesting and challenging garment designs.

A significant part of the book is devoted to clothes for special occasions and includes strapless designs for party, evening or bridalwear, the technique of ruching bodices and sleeves and the gathering of skirts to shaped seams, including the fishtail effect. The designs at the end of the book are all based on techniques previously demonstrated.

The extensive stretchwear section uses different modelling techniques, and shows how to model a wide variety of actionwear including crop tops, vests and cycling shorts, tights and unitards, swimsuits, a mini dress and a backless evening dress.

The inclusion of stretchwear and special occasion clothes will be welcomed by those working in these expanding areas of clothing construction, but has inevitably meant that other processes have been omitted. The purpose of a new book, however, is to introduce new material and any gaps in the block development section are well covered in previous books on the subject.

This book is full of guidelines rather than rules. Experimentation and experience are the best teachers; adapt and alter the methods to follow your own inspiration. I hope that *Fashion Design on the Stand* will be helpful to all those who love designing and creating beautiful clothes as a career or for their personal pleasure.

Equipment and preparation

Equipment

Modelling fabric: unbleached calico, muslin or any other inexpensive fabric which resembles the weight of the chosen garment fabric.

Cutting table: a sensible size is 3 metres (118") long by 1.5 metres (59") wide by approximately 91.5cm (36") high. This will accommodate most fabric widths and allow for a full-length evening dress. The height should be comfortable to work at when standing.

Mirror: a full-length mirror placed behind the stand or a live model enables the designer to judge the all-round effect of the garment.

Shears: for cutting fabric and scissors for cutting paper and card. Small scissors are used for snipping into seam allowances.

Tape measure.

Metre rule or yard stick and a short ruler for patternmaking.

Set square: essential for obtaining right angles on patterns and fabrics.

Pattern paper and card: for creating patterns and blocks. The paper may be plain, graph, or printed with dot and cross which provides right angles and lines to mark the grain accurately.

Tracing wheel: for transferring lines from modelled fabric to paper and for copying patterns.

French curve: useful for drawing smooth curves at the neck and armhole and on curved seams.

Pencils: hard pencils, marked H, produce fine, clear lines for pattern making. Soft pencils, marked HB are best for drawing and marking fabric.

Marking pens: water soluble pens are useful for marking toiles but leave water marks on satin and some silks. 'Fadeaway' pens leave a mark for a few hours before disappearing and are reliable for use on most fabrics.

Pins: these should be long and fine for modelling fine fabrics. Lills, very short pins, are useful for taping design lines on the stand. They sink into the surface at an angle and are easily removed by pulling the tape off the stand.

Other useful items are weights, which hold down fabric, card or patterns and prevent them moving about when being outlined; a stiletto or scriber for puncturing small holes in card; and a notcher, which clips out a small, narrow rectangle in fabric, card and patterns.

Choosing a dress stand

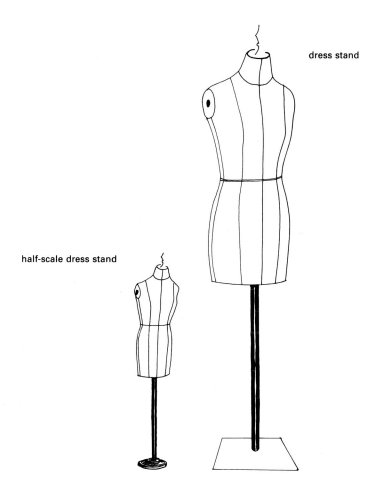

dress stand

half-scale dress stand

Stand manufacturers regularly update the shapes of stands to ensure they are appropriate for modern designs. There are various types of stand for women, men and children, as well as half-scale stands and stands with detachable arms for modelling sleeves. Women's stands are available in many shapes and sizes for dresses, skirts, trousers, swimwear, outerwear and maternity clothes.

Professional dress stands have solidly stuffed torsos, are height adjustable and are supported by a strong, heavy base. Some have retractable shoulders. The firm linen exterior of most stands is divided vertically into eight panels, providing the main seamlines on which most fitted garments are constructed.

Instructions for making a stuffed arm for modelling sleeve styles can be found on page 30.

Taking measurements

Metric Standard Measurement Chart (UK) (Read one size lower for USA)

The following measurements represent *body* sizes, not stand or *standard block* sizes. Blocks represent body size plus tolerance for movement, and represent the fit over underwear. The figures shown in the 'Movement Tolerance' (**M.T.**) column refer to the amounts already incorporated in *blocks* to allow for normal body movement when wearing garments. Increments (**Incre.**) are not always the same between all sizes, i.e. smaller sizes may be found to have less than the average and larger sizes more, according to body area. Some measurements, e.g. the wrist, tend not to increase or decrease in proportion to other girth changes. Use the size chart as a guide to girth for each size. Use *either* the Imperial Measurement chart *or* the Metric chart, not a combination of both. It is not possible to convert every figure exactly from one system to the other.

UK Body Measurements (centimetres)

Size	8	10	12	14	16	18	20	22	M.T.	Incre.	Block Size 12
Neck	34.0	35.0	36.0	37.0	38.0	39.0	41.0	42.0	-	1.0	36.0
Shoulder	11.6	11.8	12.0	12.2	12.4	12.6	12.8	13.0	-	0.2	12.0
X-back	34.0	35.0	36.0	37.0	38.0	39.0	40.0	41.0	1.6	1.0	37.6
X-chest	31.5	32.5	33.5	34.5	35.5	36.5	37.5	38.5	0.6	1.0	34.1
Underarm	74.0	78.0	82.0	86.0	90.0	94.0	98.0	102.0	5.0	4.0	87.0
Bust level	77.0	82.0	87.0	92.0	97.0	102.0	107.0	112.0	10.0	5.0	97.0
Under Bust	61.0	66.0	71.0	76.0	81.0	86.0	91.0	96.0	5.0	5.0	76.0
Bust span	16.8	18.0	19.2	20.4	21.6	22.8	24.0	25.2	-	1.2	19.2
Armhole	38.6	40.6	42.6	44.6	46.6	48.6	50.6	52.6	-	2.0	42.6
Waist	55.0	60.0	65.0	70.0	75.0	80.0	85.0	90.0 skirts trousers dresses	1cm 1cm 4cm	5.0	66.0 66.0 69.0
High hip	80.0	84.0	88.0	92.0	96.0	100.0	104.0	108.0	5	4.0	91.0
Hip	86.0	90.0	94.0	98.0	102.0	106.0	110.0	114.0	5	4–5	99.0
Bicep	26.0	27.0	28.0	29.0	30.0	31.0	32.0	33.0	5	1.0	28.0
Elbow	22.2	24.0	25.8	27.6	29.4	31.2	34.0	35.8	5	1.8	30.8
Wrist	15.0	15.5	16.0	16.5	17.0	17.5	18.0	18.5	6.5	0.8	22.5
Thigh	48.0	51.0	54.0	57.0	60.0	63.0	66.0	69.0	-	3.0	54.0
Knee	32.2	32.6	34.0	35.4	36.8	38.2	39.6	41.0	6	1.4	40.0
Calf	30.2	31.6	33.0	34.4	35.8	37.2	38.6	40.0	-	1.4	33.0
Ankle	21.8	22.4	23.0	23.6	24.2	24.8	25.4	26.0	9	0.6	32.0
Height	157.2	159.6	162.0	164.4	166.8	169.2	171.6	173.0	-	2.4	162.0
Nape/ waist	38.8	39.4	40.0	40.6	41.2	41.8	42.4	43.0	-	0.6	40.0
Nape/ ground	135.8	137.9	140.0	142.1	144.2	146.3	148.4	150.5	-	2.1	140.0
Waist to hip	19.4	19.7	20.0	20.3	20.6	20.9	21.2	21.5	-	0.3	20.0

									M.T.	Incre.	Block
Waist/ knee	56.4	57.2	58.0	58.8	60.6	61.4	62.2	70.0	-	0.8	58.0
Waist/ floor	97.4	98.7	103.0	104.3	105.6	106.9	108.2	109.5	-	1.3	100.0
Outer sleeve	56.2	57.1	58.0	58.9	59.8	60.7	61.6	62.5	-	0.9	58.0
Nape/ nipple	32.3	33.7	34.5	35.9	37.3	38.7	40.1	41.5	-	1.4	34.0
Body rise	26.8	27.2	28.0	28.8	29.6	30.4	31.2	32.1	*	0.8	29.0
Crotch length	61.0	63.5	66.0	68.5	71.0	73.5	76.0	78.5	**	2.5	66.0

* Included (measured in seated position)   ** Included (may be measured in seated or in standing position)

Imperial Standard Measurement Chart (UK) (Read one size lower for USA)
Body Measurements (inches)

Size	8	10	12	14	16	18	20	22	M.T.	Incre.	Block
Neck	$13^7/_8$	14	$14^1/_8$	14	$14^7/_8$	15	$15^5/_8$	16	-	$^3/_8$	$14^1/_8$
Shoulder	4	$4^3/_8$	4	$5^1/_8$	5	$5^7/_8$	6	$6^5/_8$	-	$^3/_8$	4
X-back	$13^3/_8$	$13^7/_8$	$14^3/_8$	$14^7/_8$	$15^3/_8$	$15^7/_8$	$16^3/_8$	$16^7/_8$	$^5/_8$	-	15
X-chest	$12^1/_8$	$12^5/_8$	$13^1/_8$	$14^5/_8$	$15^1/_8$	$15^5/_8$	$16^1/_8$	$16^5/_8$	-	-	$13^3/_8$
Underarm	29	30	32	33	35	36	38	39	-	1	32
Bust	$30^5/_8$	$32^5/_8$	$34^5/_8$	$36^5/_8$	$38^5/_8$	$40^5/_8$	$42^5/_8$	$44^5/_8$	4	2	$38^5/_8$
Under bust	24	26	28	30	32	34	36	38	-	2	28
Bust span	6	7	7	8	8	9	9	10	-	-	7
Armhole	15	16	16	17	18	19	19	20	-	-	16
Waist	22	24	26	28	30	32	34	36 skirts trousers dresses	- $^3/_8$ $^3/_8$ 1	2	- $27^1/_8$ $27^1/_8$ 28
High hip	$30^5/_8$	$32^5/_8$	$34^5/_8$	$36^5/_8$	$38^5/_8$	$40^5/_8$	$42^5/_8$	$44^5/_8$	1	2	$36^1/_8$
Hip	33	35	37	39	41	43	45	47	2	2	39
Bicep	9	9	10	11	12	12	13	14	2	-	12
Elbow	$8^5/_8$	$9^1/_8$	$9^7/_8$	$10^5/_8$	$11^1/_8$	$11^7/_8$	$12^5/_8$	$13^1/_8$	2	-	$11^7/_8$
Wrist	6	6	6	$6^5/_8$	7	$7^3/_8$	7	$8^1/_8$	2	$^3/_8$	8
Thigh	18	20	21	22	23	25	26	27	-	1	21
Knee	12	13	13	14	14	15	15	16	2	-	16
Calf	12	12	13	13	14	14	15	15	-	-	13
Ankle	8	8	9	9	9	9	10	10	3	+	12
Height	62	63	64	65	66	67	68	69	-	1	64
Nape/waist	15	$15^7/_8$	$16^1/_8$	$16^3/_8$	$16^5/_8$	$16^7/_8$	$17^1/_8$	$17^3/_8$	-	-	$16^1/_8$
Nape/ground	54	55	56	56	57	58	59	50	-	+	56
Waist/hip	$7^5/_8$	7	$7^7/_8$	8	$8^1/_8$	8	$8^5/_8$	8	-	$^1/_8$	$7^7/_8$
Waist/knee	23	23	23	23	24	24	24	24	-	-	23
Waist/floor	39	40	40	41	41	42	42	43	-	-	40
Outer sleeve	$22^1/_8$	22	$22^7/_8$	23	$23^5/_8$	24	$24^3/_8$	24	-	$^3/_8$	$22^7/_8$
Nape/nipple	12	13	13	14	14	15	15	16	-	-	13
Body rise	10	10	11	11	12	12	13	13	*	-	11
Crotch length	24	25	26	27	28	29	30	31	**	1	27

* Included (measured in seated position)   ** Included (may be measured in seated or in standing position)

10

across back

shoulder to wrist

armhole girth

shoulder

bicep girth

elbow girth

forearm girth

wrist girth

neck girth

side neck to waist

across chest

underarm

bust

under bust

nape to back waist

waist

high hip

hip

nape to floor

front neck to waist

mid thigh girth

knee girth

calf girth

ankle girth

Two sets of measurements are in common use: standard and individual. Standard measurements are obtained from charts, and are used in mass production to create garments at competitive prices, in commercial paper patterns for home dressmakers, and in teaching. Individual measurements apply when garments are made to personal measurements.

Most designers are familiar with standard body sizes and the amount of tolerance which should be added for normal body movement when working with woven fabrics. This will vary according to the purpose of the garment and the fabrics chosen. More allowance for active movement is needed in sportswear, dancing and work clothes, less for those worn for sedentary occupations. Woven fabrics have intrinsic qualities and, in order to create beautiful and comfortable clothes, the difference between body measurements and garment measurements must be understood and accepted.

Fabrics

Dress design begins with fabric. Fabric is often created with particular designers in mind who then interpret it into fashion shapes.

The colour, texture and weight of fabrics determine the silhouette and the design lines of the garment. The handle - the way a fabric hangs, drapes and moves - suggests both possibilities and limitations to the designer whose instinct and experience will lead to choices compatible with both fabric and design. When sketches precede the choice of fabric it is not always possible to find the right fabric to achieve the original design. When fabric choice precedes the sketch or even the idea itself, the fabric characteristics are instrumental in the design concept and in the hands of an experienced designer are more likely to work to perfection.

Many designers prefer to work with plain rather than patterned, and knitted rather than woven fabrics. With patterned fabrics, the size of the pattern and the pattern repeat must be considered in relation to the garment.

Most prints obscure design lines and can limit the designer's imagination by preventing the use of certain lines which would interrupt the fabric pattern. For this reason the majority of collections feature unpatterned fabrics in clear, stunning colours which show off the design seams and clever cut and emphasize the silhouette.

Garment design is inspired by fabric which is studied in relation to the type of client and occasion for which it will be worn. With experience and confidence the fabric may be cut directly on the stand but it is usual to make up a trial garment (a toile) in an inexpensive substitute fabric to evaluate the design and make any minor adjustments. After this, a pattern is made from the toile and is used to cut out the expensive fabric.

Many fabrics come into the 'special' category: silk, satin, lace, brocade, taffeta, chiffon, *crepe-de-chine* and velvet. Special finishes include embroidered, beaded, sequinned and metallic fabrics and may be woven or knitted. Added to these must be the increasing variety of stretch fabrics such as silk jersey and stretch lace designed for special occasion wear.

The fabric for making the preliminary toile should be as close as possible in weight and texture to the fabric to be used in the actual garment. The basic blocks and most of the exercises in this book may be modelled in medium and lightweight calico. Cotton jersey is suitable for making the toiles in the stretch section.

Padding up the stand

Stands are constructed to body measurements, not garment sizes. Garments made from woven fabrics must be cut larger than the body to permit comfortable movement. Allow for this difference by padding up the stand to the size required.

In mass production, standard size dress stands are padded up to include both tolerance for body movement and extra 'design ease' where required. Some large clothing firms have stands constructed to include tolerances to their own specification.

Individual designers and small companies use standard size stands and pad them up as needed. Some couturiers have special stands made for important clients which eliminates the need for fittings.

The amount of tolerance needed for body movement depends on the type of garment and the degree of 'fit' needed to create the required silhouette. Work clothes demand more 'ease' than strapless evening dresses, but both must be comfortable. In addition to this is 'designer ease', the often considerable amount of extra fabric needed to achieve the 'look'. As a guide, pad up the stand to allow for body movement and include the designer ease in the modelling. The amount needed will become apparent in the look of the garment during modelling and depends on knowledge and experience of interpreting designs.

For standard measurements allow the following increments which remain constant for all sizes whether increasing or decreasing.

Skirt and trouser waist: 1cm (½") Dress waist: 4cm(1⅝") Bust: 10cm (4") Hips: 5cm (2") Across back: 1.6cm (⅝") Across chest: 0.6cm (¼") Bicep: 5cm (2") Elbow: 5cm (2") Knee: 6cm (2¼")

(a)

(b)

(a) Use strips of sheet wadding to increase the overall size of the waist and hips. For the bust contours cut thinner layers to different sizes and layer one over another. Pin the first piece and the remaining layers will adhere to each other. Cover with a piece of lightweight calico which will stretch to the bust shape.

(b) To raise the shoulder level use a shoulder pad or layers of wadding. To re-position the waist and hiplines, fill in the hollow gap in the stand waistline, measure the correct nape to back waist distance and tape the new waistline. The hip level will move up or down accordingly. Thin out the wadding at upper and lower edges.

Taping the stand

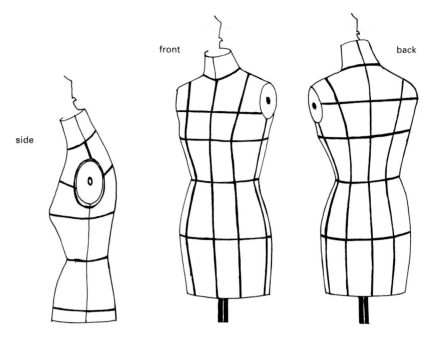

Using narrow black tape to emphasize the main seamlines of the stand allows them to be seen through the modelling fabric, so clearly establishing the correct seam and dart positions when modelling the blocks. This is a useful device for beginners until they are familiar with the stand and able to detect the stand seamlines with the fingertips. Taping the correct horizontal lines for bust, waist and hiplines helps to keep the horizontal grainline of the fabric level with that of the stand.

With experience this process can be omitted, although taping the stand for necklines and other design lines is an essential technique at all stages of modelling. Tape can be fixed to the stand with lills which easily pull away when not needed.

Bust, waist and hiplines start and finish at centre back.
All horizontal lines must be parallel to the floor.
Panel seamlines start at the lower edge of the stand and continue over the shoulder down to the other side
All vertical lines end at the lower edge of the stand.
Use masking tape or a tack to secure vertical lines beneath the stand.

Work in the following order in order to conceal raw edges:

Centre front: from base of neck.
Side seams: from underarm point.
Panel lines: find centre of tape, pin to shoulder, leaving ends free. Pin one end down back, then one down front of stand.
Shoulder seam: from side neck point to shoulder point.
Bustline: from centre back, in circle over front bust points.
Waistline: around narrowest part of waist.
Hipline: 20cm (8") below waistline.
Across backline: 10cm (4") down from nape (at right angles to centre back).
Across chestline: 10cm (4") down from base of neck (at right angles to centre front).
The armhole ends of these lines mark the back and front 'pitch' marks for balancing the sleeves into the armholes.
Centre back: from nape.
Neck line: start at centre back, follow neck curve, overlap tape at centre back.
Armhole: minimum armhole circumference: 42cm (16½"): 20cm (8") at back, 22cm (8½") at front. Lower the stand underarm point by approximately 2cm (¾"). Armhole width: 11cm (4¼").

Modelling basic blocks

Blocks, also known as shells or templates, are shaped by manipulating fabric or paper to the contours of the dress stand. This provides a basic pattern which may be developed into different garment designs. The fabric or paper shape is then transferred to firm plastic or card to make a permanent template for future use.

Not every new garment design needs to be modelled from the beginning. Most styles develop from a basic identity, featuring darts or panel lines, and require only minor changes such as a different neckline, fastening or hem length. For many designs, the time taken to repeat the basic garment shape can be saved by starting from one of the primary blocks. A set of primary blocks includes front and back bodice; sleeve; and front and back skirt, each of which lends itself to many variations.

Main points to remember when modelling a set of interchangeable primary blocks:

The sleeves must fit the bodice armholes. The bodice and skirt waistlines must match. The waist of a fitted skirt is not the same as the lower half of a dress with a waistline seam, the latter is looser.

Most garment designs are symmetrical and are modelled on one half (the right hand side) of the stand. This produces a half-pattern which, when cut in double fabric, fits both sides of the body. Asymmetric styles and modelling directly in the final fabric demand the use of both sides of the dress stand.

The Figures given in the exercises in this book use standard size 12. Please refer to the size charts for all other sizes.

This section describes three different styles of bodice block, matching skirt blocks and a sleeve block, together with instructions for making them into permanent patterns.

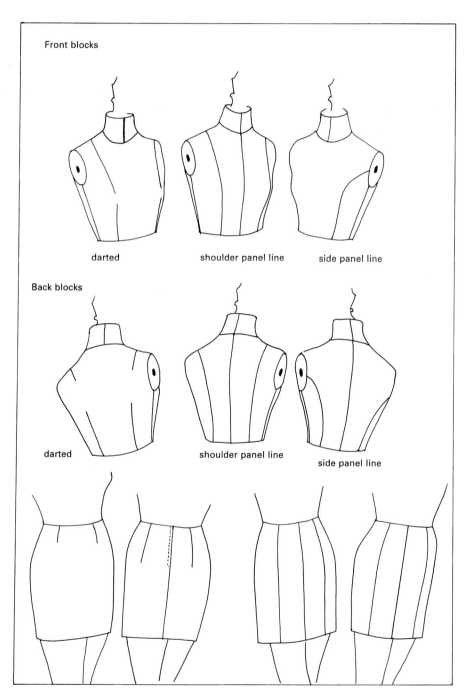

Front blocks

darted   shoulder panel line   side panel line

Back blocks

darted   shoulder panel line   side panel line

front and back darted skirt   back and front panel line skirt

Bodice blocks to waist level

The classic bodice blocks offer three distinct looks: darted; panel lines from shoulder to waist and side panels (shaped seams from armhole to waist). Bodice blocks may extend from shoulder to waist, to hip level, between the waist and hip and above the waist ('cropped'.) When taken below mid-thigh they become dress blocks. The waist length blocks form the bodice for dresses with a waist seam; blocks extending below the waist can become blouses, dresses with a dropped waist or jackets. Instructions will be given for all three classic blocks. The techniques involved are the basis of all fitted styles and should be mastered before attempting those shown in the advanced section.

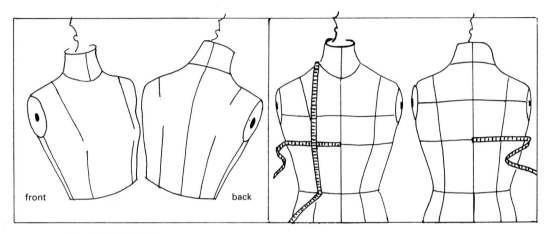

front   back

DARTED BLOCK TO WAIST LEVEL

(a) To find the fabric length required, measure from the neck point on the front of the stand over the bust point to the front waist, 44.5cm (17½"), and add 10cm (4"). Total = 54.5cm (21½"). To find the fabric width required, measure from centre front to side seam on bustline and add 5cm (2") and then from centre back to side seam, also adding 5cm (2"). Added together, these give the total width of material needed for modelling the front and back half blocks to waist level. Snip off the selvedge and tear off this length.

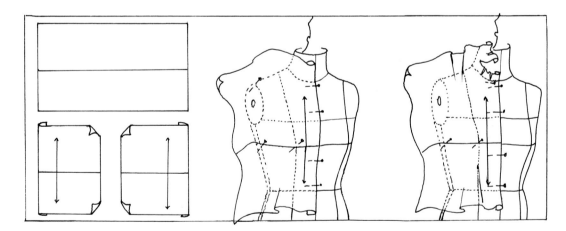

(b) Mark a horizontal line for bust level 30cm (11¾") down from the top edge of fabric. Cut off two strips for the back and front of block. Trim off the fabric selvedges and turn under a 2cm (1") fold for centre front and centre back.

(c) Align the vertical straight grain fold of fabric to centre front stand seamline, matching bust level lines of fabric and stand. Pin fabric to centre front stand seamline, allowing it to extend beyond shoulder and waist. Smooth fabric across to side seam and attach with anchor pins at bust point, side seam and shoulder to control fabric temporarily.

(d) Remove anchor pin at shoulder and smooth fabric up from the bust level. The surplus fabric between neck point and shoulder point will form the shoulder dart. To shape the neckline, control the fabric below the neckline with one hand, cut away obvious surplus fabric, snip to neck seamline at 1cm (⅜") intervals and pin just below seamline. Reduce seam allowance to 1.5cm (½").

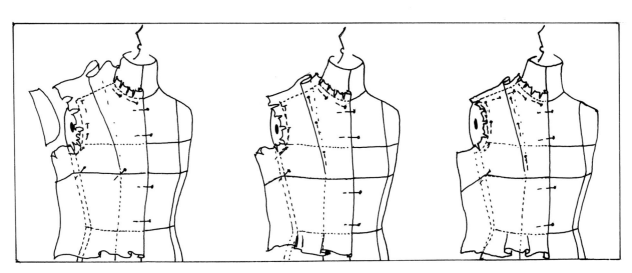

(e) Cut away surplus fabric in the armhole area. Snip to seamline. Shape armhole as for neckline. Reduce seam allowance to 1.5cm (½"). Smooth the remainder of fabric in the shoulder area towards the neckline. The surplus fabric will become the shoulder dart.

(f) Remove anchor pin from bust point. Fold a large dart from shoulder to within 1.5cm (½") of bust point in line with the panel seam on the stand. Fold dart under towards neckline. Pin.

(g) Check smoothness of fabric between dart and armhole. If corrections are necessary, un-pin, smooth excess fabric into the dart and re-pin. Pin the shoulder seam from neck point to shoulder point. Trim seam allowance.

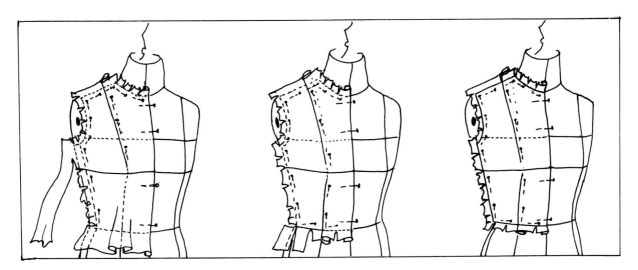

(h) Remove side seam anchor pin and smooth fabric below the bustline towards the waist. Allow surplus fabric to fall below bust point. This will become the waist dart. Remove anchor pin and pin side seam from underarm to waist, trimming surplus fabric and snipping to seamline.

(i) Snip the fabric below the waist up to waist level. Form the waist dart, stopping 1.5cm (½") from bust point, and fold it towards centre front. Trim the surplus fabric below waistline and pin waist seamline.

(j) Mark seamlines and dart edges. Leave front toile on the stand until back is completed.

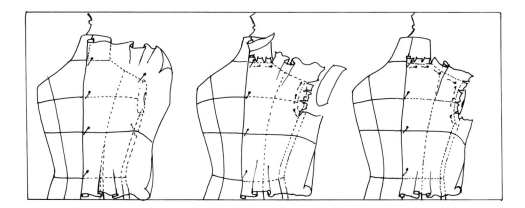

(a) For the back, pin the fold of fabric to the centre back of the stand, matching the bustlines of fabric and stand. Anchor pin at the shoulder and side seam.

(b) Shape the back neckline and armhole as before, snipping to the seamline. Pin on seamlines and trim seam allowances to 1.5cm (½").

(c) Form a back shoulder dart about 7.5cm (3") long, in line with the stand panel seam. Fold it towards centre back and pin. Pin the shoulder seam and trim seam allowance.

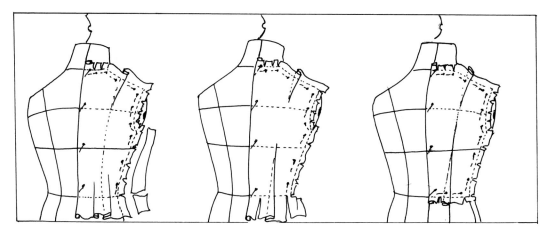

(d) Allow surplus fabric to fall below the shoulder blade. Snip and pin at side seam.

(e) Snip the fabric below the waist up to seamline. Form the surplus fabric into a waist dart 15-18cm long (6-7") in line with the stand panel line and turned towards the centre back. Pin.

(f) Trim surplus fabric at waistline and pin.

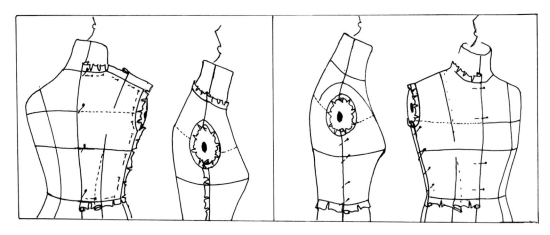

(g) Mark seamlines and dart edges. Remove pins at shoulder. Pin shoulder seams together, folding under the front seam allowance and pinning it to the back along the marked seamline. The seam should be in line with the stand shoulder seamline.

(h) Complete side seam as for shoulder seam. Bust level lines on back and front blocks should meet and the side seam should match that of the stand. The bodice block is now ready for trueing.

Trueing the block

Remove the modelled block from the stand, take out any remaining pins and press flat without distorting the shape. It is possible to use these fabric sections as a pattern to cut out a garment, but because blocks can be used indefinitely as the basis for future designs, it is practical to copy them on to card or plastic to preserve their shape and firm edges.

When copying the blocks on to card, disregard the rather ragged seam allowances. It is more accurate to add these directly on to the paper or card, if at all. Because seam allowances will vary, some designers prefer to mark the correct amounts directly on to the fabric when cutting it out. A 1-1.5cm (½ - ¾") seam allowance is adequate for the outer edges of blocks. This allows them to be tacked up and put on the stand for evaluation or further development.

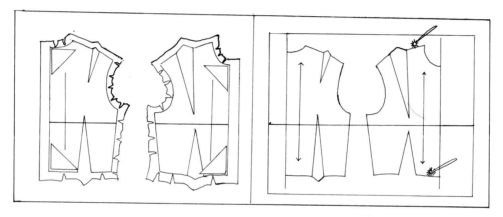

(a) Use a ruler to straighten or 'true' the shoulder seams, side seams and dart edges, a set square to check that intersections are at right angles to each other, and a curve to obtain a smooth run on neck and armhole seams. Check that the side seams are of equal length and that the back and front shoulder seams will match when the darts are closed. Draw in straight grain lines parallel to the centre front and centre back.

(b) To transfer the fabric sections to paper, draw parallel vertical lines on the paper, with a horizontal line at right angles between them for the bust level and a space all round for seam allowance. Place the front and back fabric pattern sections on to the paper, matching the bust levels centre front and centre back and weigh down in place (using pins will distort the shape). Trace off the trued seamlines, dartlines and grainlines and remove the toile from the paper.

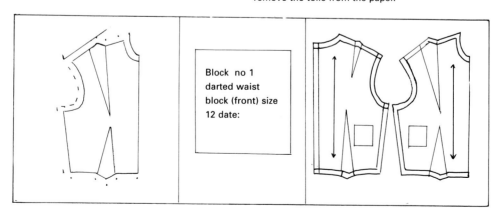

Block no 1
darted waist
block (front) size
12 date:

(c) Measure and mark the required seam allowances on to all edges of the block pattern except the centre front and mark in the straight grainlines. Add a label with information such as size, name of the piece and how many to cut.

Shoulder panel block

This second waist block is modelled omitting darts. The three-dimensional shape is achieved by using the vertical seamlines of the stand to create an eight-panelled bodice. It will be seven-panelled if either the centre front or centre back is placed on a fold. The panels can be modelled in any order, and these exercises provide a variety of approaches.

SHOULDER PANEL BLOCK

20

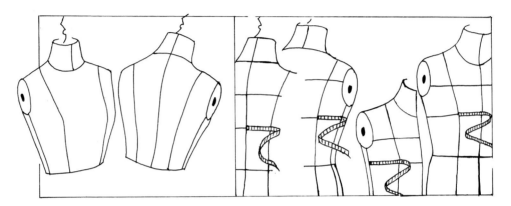

Front, back.

(a) Measure the individual stand panels at the widest part (bustline). The side panels are wider than the centre panels.

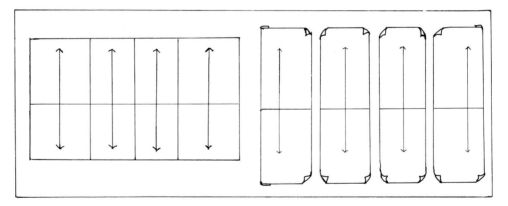

(b) Cut a 52cm (20½") length of fabric. Mark a horizontal line for the bustline level across the entire piece.

(c) Cut into four lengthwise strips. Mark a vertical grainline through the centre of each strip. Fold under 2cm (¾") for centre front and centre back.

NEW TECHNIQUES

Modelling with narrow strips of fabric
Maintaining a smooth seamline through the bust curve

DESIGN NOTE

Panel lines are continuous seams which run from the upper edge (the shoulder or armhole in bodices, the waist in skirts) to the lower edge of a garment. They may be broken by a waistline seam in a dress, but when undisturbed by any horizontal seam they are known as 'princess lines'. Because of the vertical emphasis in the design, panels give the illusion of height, whereas horizontal lines break the garment into layers and appear to shorten the wearer.

(d)   (e)   (f)   (g)

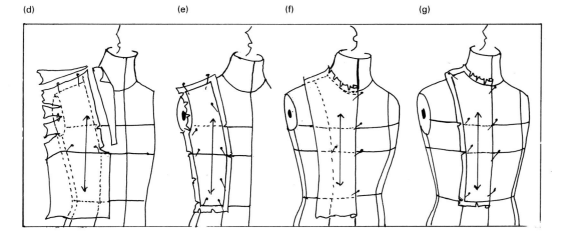

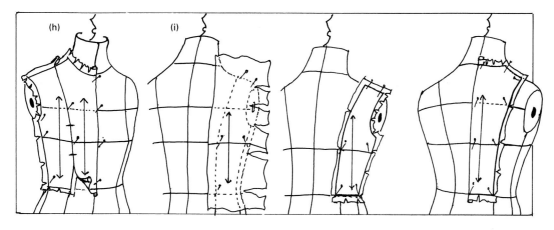

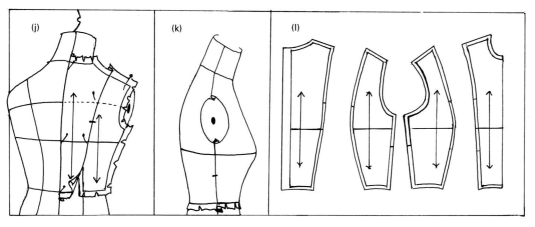

(d) Front side panel: Match the marked horizontal line on the fabric to the taped bustline of the stand. Anchor pin at side seam and bust point. Smooth fabric above the bust upwards to front shoulder. Cut into the armhole area to prevent the fabric puckering. Pin at shoulder point and top of panel.

(e) Pin from bust point up to top of panel line, trimming and snipping the seamline to release tension. Complete armhole shaping. Reduce seam allowances to 1.5cm (½"). Smooth fabric below bustline down to waist. Complete the panel seam, side seam and waistline. Mark the seamlines, following the tape on the stand. Remove pins from the panel line and replace them away from the seamline. Pull the fabric back to allow work on the centre front panel.

(f) Centre front panel: Pin vertical straight grain of fabric to the centre front seamline of stand, matching the marked bustline on the fabric to the stand bustline. Use an anchor pin at the bust point. Complete neckline shaping.

(g) Snip to bustline, and pin panel line up to shoulder, then down to waist following the panel seamline. Reduce seam allowance to 1.5cm (½"). Mark the seamline.

(h) Take out the panel line pins and smooth the side panel towards the centre front. Fold under the centre panel seamline on the marked line and pin to the marked seamline of the side panel. Remove surplus pins from the side panel. Mark notches 4cm (1½") above and below the bust point.

(i) Model the back bodice following the panel lines.

(j) Fold panel seam allowances towards the centre back.

(k) Complete side and shoulder seams as for the darted block. Mark all seams and add notch marks to the back panel and side seams.

(l) Remove the toile from the stand. Iron the panels flat and true the lines, checking that horizontal lines and notches meet accurately. Transfer the pattern to paper or card for future use.

Side panel line to waist block

This block is the third of the three classic bodice shapes which are used as a basis for further styling. In the previous blocks, the suppression of surplus fabric in the waist and shoulder areas was achieved by the use of darts or vertical panel lines which follow the curve of the body from shoulder to waist over the bust. Creating a seamline which starts in the armhole and travels in a pronounced curve over the bust point calls for greater control over the fabric grain. For the first time, the familiar landmarks of the stand panel seams will be ignored above the bust point and a new design line introduced.

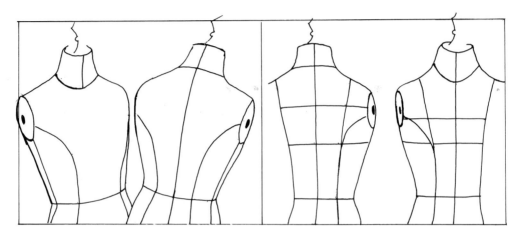

SIDE PANEL LINE TO WAIST BLOCK

(a) Leave the stand taped as for previous blocks. The tape above bust level on front and back of the stand will be ignored. For the side panel, tape the stand from mid-armhole to waist in a curve going through the bust point on the front and in a less pronounced curve from armhole to waist on the back.

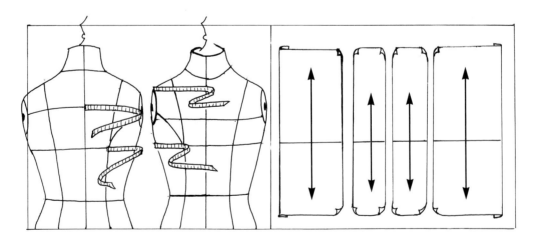

(b) Measure the widths of these four panels. The centre front and back panels both extend to the shoulder points and are wider and longer than the side panels.

(c) Prepare a length of fabric with clear grain lines as for the previous block. Mark bustline and straight grain lines.

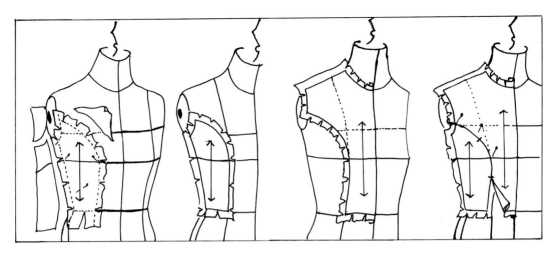

(d) Side front panel: Model as for the previous block, but follow the new taped line from armhole to waist. The armhole section will be quite shallow.

(e) Centre front panel: Model the panel in the same way as the previous block, but take the upper section across to the armhole following the new panel line.

(f) Model the back sections in the same order as the previous block, taking the centre back panel across to the shoulder. Mark all seamlines and notches.

(g) Remove the toile from the stand, true lines and complete as for previous blocks.

DESIGN NOTE

Taking the design seam or dart away from the shoulder area makes possible a far wider scope of interesting necklines. However it is quite common practice to design low, wide necklines in shoulder panel line styles, particularly in party and evening wear.

NEW TECHNIQUES

Creating and taping a new design line
Modelling to a pronounced curve
Transferring three-dimensional control to the armhole area

Alternative dart positions

Fabric is cut to fit the widest areas of the body: the bust and hips. This leaves a surplus in narrower areas such as at the waist and shoulders. Darts and seams are the main techniques used to create garments which follow the three-dimensional shape of the human form. Gathers and pleats are other ways of controlling surplus fabric but are more suitable for creating shapes which are narrow at the top and wide at the hem, such as full skirts. The combination of such techniques for controlling or releasing fabric enables the designer to create a variety of garment silhouettes. The position of darts is as prone to changes in fashion as any aspect of design.

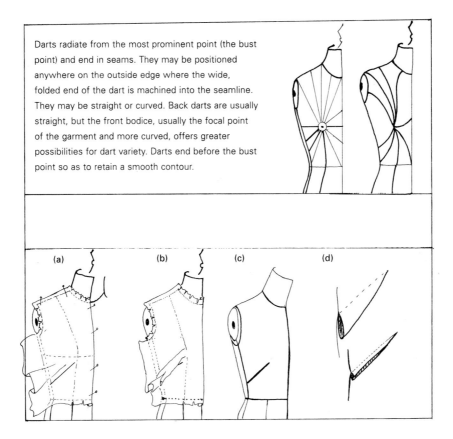

Darts radiate from the most prominent point (the bust point) and end in seams. They may be positioned anywhere on the outside edge where the wide, folded end of the dart is machined into the seamline. They may be straight or curved. Back darts are usually straight, but the front bodice, usually the focal point of the garment and more curved, offers greater possibilities for dart variety. Darts end before the bust point so as to retain a smooth contour.

(a)   (b)   (c)   (d)

(a) Tape the new dart position and model as before until the neckline is shaped. Complete armhole and shoulder seam. Surplus fabric is directed towards the side seam.
(b) Form surplus fabric into a large dart from the side seam towards the bust point and pin.
(c) Outside appearance of dart.
(d) Two darts in one can cause too much bulk. Trim to 1cm (½″) to form a dart seam.

NEW TECHNIQUES

Discovering new dart positions for achieving a three-dimensional shape
Controlling fabric on the bias
Practising straight and curved darts
Controlling all surplus fabric in a single dart

24

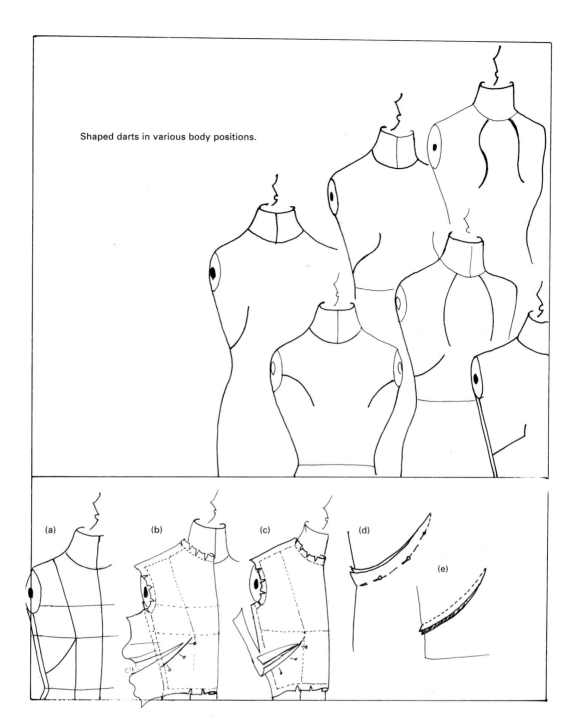

Shaped darts in various body positions.

(a) Tape a curved dart.
(b) Model as for the straight French dart, but pin the dartline leaving surplus material above. Mark dartline. Cut into the fabric as shown.

(c) Smooth surplus fabric to dartline and mark dartline position, Trim to 1.5cm (½").
(d) Repin the dartline.
(e) Sew the dartline.

DESIGN NOTE

Dart positions are dictated by fashion, fabric and fit.
Fashion: When close-fitting styles are in fashion, designers use straight, curved and variously shaped darts, prominently placed, to create the line.
Fabric: Darts show up better on plain coloured fabrics and can destroy the flow of patterned fabrics by cutting through the motifs.
Fit: The triangular shape of the dart makes it a useful device for eliminating surplus fabric, releasing it gradually to create a smooth surface over the body's contours.
Darts transform the two-dimensional fabric into a three-dimensional garment.

Sleeveless bodices

The basic bodice block armholes are designed to accept sleeves but the armholes are too wide and the underarm too low for most sleeveless styles which fit closer to the body. For sleeveless styles there is no need to model the blocks again. Make the following adjustments to the paper pattern developed from the original blocks.

Trace back and front block patterns on to pattern paper. To tighten the side seam mark a new underarm point 1.5cm (½") in from the underarm point and raise it 1.5cm (½"). Connect this point to the original side seam at waist. Re-draw the lower armhole.

Shoulder seams can be narrowed and armholes lowered instead of raised. Side seams always need to be tightened. Front armholes may also be tightened by taking a 1.5cm (½") dart from armhole to bust point. Re-direct this amount into the waist dart or panel line.

Model facings about 5cm (2") wide to incorporate neck and armhole areas.
The straight grain should be parallel to centre back and centre front respectively.

DESIGN NOTE

The high underarm is common for daywear such as sleeveless blouses and dresses. A lower cut armhole is often used in party and evening dresses, and may reach to the waist. A close body fit is essential unless used in a floaty layer over a close-fitting foundation as often found in costumes for dancing and ice-skating.

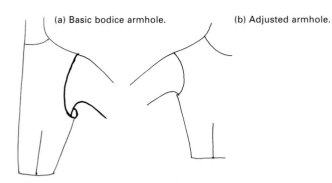

(a) Basic bodice armhole.　　　　(b) Adjusted armhole.

(c) Tightening and raising the side seam and armhole.

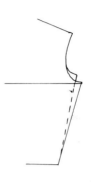

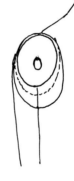

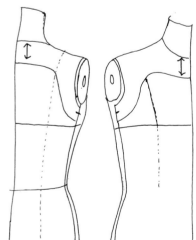

(d) Side view of stand showing normal, lower armhole for sleeve and higher armhole for sleeveless styles.

(e) Blocks have no facings. Model facings for sleeveless styles directly on to the stand when modelling the garment design.

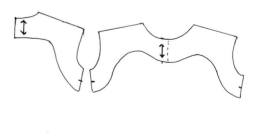

Extended blocks

Blocks constructed to any level below the waistline are not simply extended waist blocks. They do not 'nip in' the waist to the same degree as blocks ending at the waistline. The double-ended 'fish' dart is used on longer blocks. This is narrowest at the waist level to allow a degree of tolerance, with the widest part of the dart a little above the normal waist. The side seam is less fitted to avoid it riding up when the arm is lifted.

It is useful to model the blocks to hip level to learn how to handle the 'fish' dart and to create extra tolerance in the waist area.

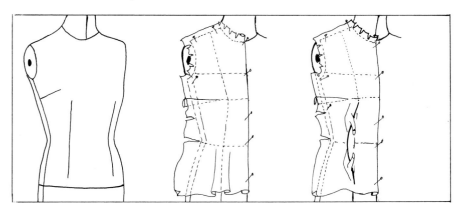

HIP BLOCK WITH FISH DARTS

(a) Model bodice, completing the shoulder and armhole. Make a small bust level dart.

(b) Pick up a long dart on the panel line, but make it less fitted than on the waist block.

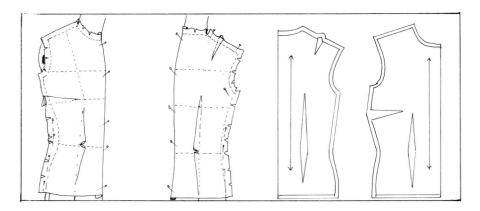

(c) Snip the dart at the waist curve. Allow a little tolerance between side seam and front dart. Re-pin side seam.

(d) Complete back.

(e) Final pattern.

NEW TECHNIQUES

Modelling a double dart
Introducing extra tolerance

All waist blocks may be extended to become blouses, tunics and mini-, knee-, calf-
and ankle-length dresses, and may include a variety of darts or panel lines.

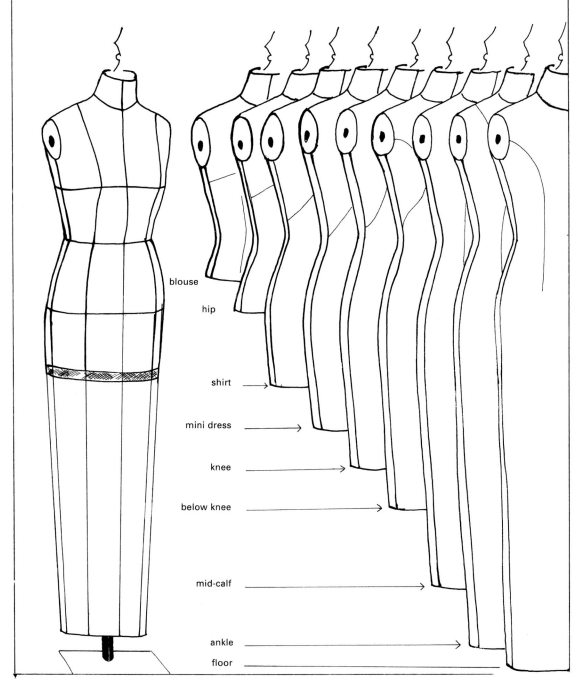

stand extended to ankle

blouse

hip

shirt

mini dress

knee

below knee

mid-calf

ankle

floor

DESIGN NOTE

The hip-length block is the basis for designing blouses, jackets,
dresses without a waistline seam and the shaped and 'dropped'
waistline seams seen frequently in evening, party and bridalwear.
All below-knee lengths require additional 'walking room'.

Making a fabric arm

Detachable arms may be bought for dress stands and are essential for modelling sleeves. Making a fabric arm of your own gives one which is more flexible and can be moved into many positions. The quarter-scale pattern below is for the right sleeve. For a pair, cut in double fabric. The arm may be pinned to the stand shoulder or used independently.

Enlarge the sleeve pattern to four times its size and add 1.5cm (½") seam allowance. Each square is equivalent to 1cm (⅜"). Cut the circles for shoulder and wrist. The flap is for pinning the arm to the stand. Mark in all lines and notches and make up as instructed.

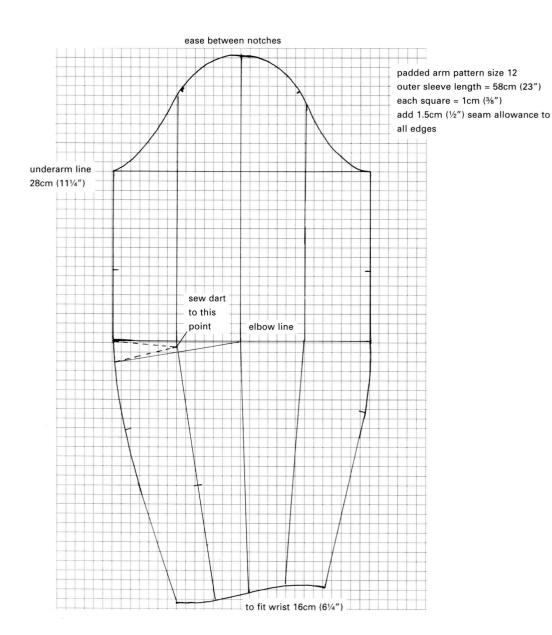

ease between notches

padded arm pattern size 12
outer sleeve length = 58cm (23")
each square = 1cm (⅜")
add 1.5cm (½") seam allowance to
all edges

underarm line
28cm (11¼")

sew dart
to this
point

elbow line

to fit wrist 16cm (6¼")

Use narrow black tape or fabric marker to mark the lines of the pattern and wadding to pad the arm. Mark or tape the vertical lines and elbow line. Machine two rows of large stitches either side of the fitting line between the dots on the sleeve head. Pull the lower (bobbin) threads up to create the top of the sleeve shape.

On the wrong side, machine the elbow dart, or ease if preferred.

Machine seam from underarm to wrist. Press seam open.

Pin and machine (hand-sew if easier) the wrist circle to the narrow end of the sleeve.

Stuff the arm with wadding.

With right sides together, machine the curved edge of the flap. Bag out and press.

On the right side of the sleeve head, position the flap between notches, pin and machine on seamline. With the flap remaining on the outside, pin and hand-sew the top arm circle to close the arm.

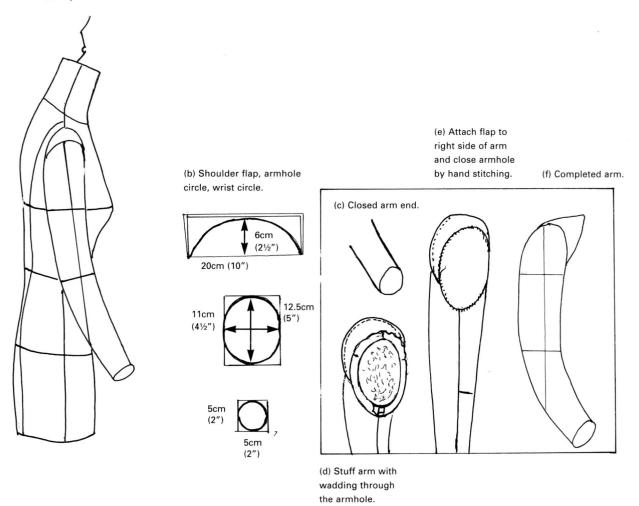

(a) Separate arm attached to stand shoulder.

(b) Shoulder flap, armhole circle, wrist circle.

6cm (2½")

20cm (10")

11cm (4½")   12.5cm (5")

5cm (2")

5cm (2")

(e) Attach flap to right side of arm and close armhole by hand stitching.

(f) Completed arm.

(c) Closed arm end.

(d) Stuff arm with wadding through the armhole.

Skirts

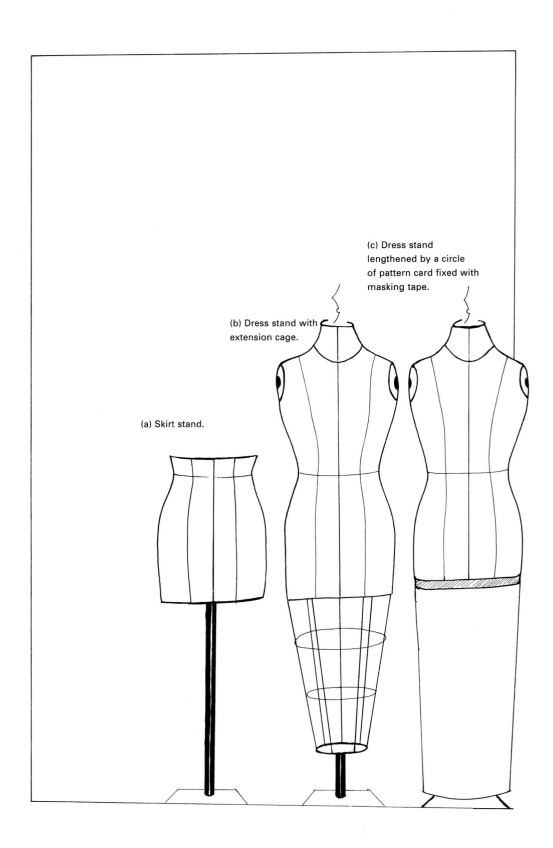

(c) Dress stand lengthened by a circle of pattern card fixed with masking tape.

(b) Dress stand with extension cage.

(a) Skirt stand.

Straight skirt with darts and back vent

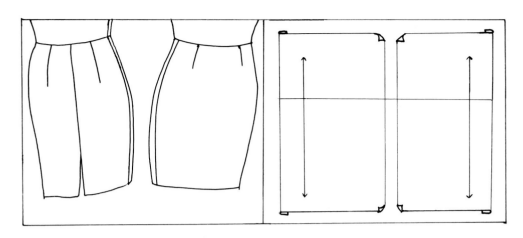

(a) Back and front of straight skirt with darts and back vent.

(b) Cut the skirt length plus 10cm (4″) from the fabric. Cut two strips, each ¼ hip measurement + 5cm (2″). Mark the hip level and straight grain. Fold under outer edges for centre back and centre front.

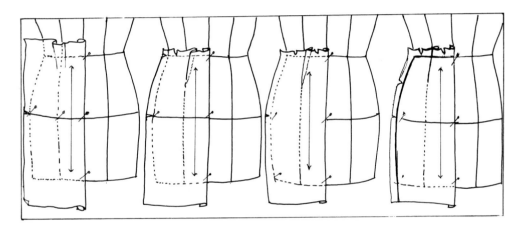

(c) To model the front skirt, pin the fabric to the stand, matching hip levels.

(d) Pin the side seam above the hip and fold surplus fabric into a waist dart 9cm (3½″) long on the panel line.

(e) Fold dart towards centre front and complete side seam.

(f) Mark seamlines and dart edges.

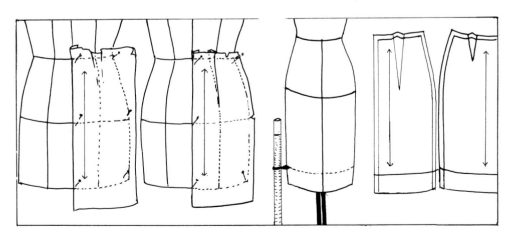

(g) Model the back skirt, leaving surplus fabric above the hip in the panel seam area.

(h) Fold and pin a dart 14cm (5½″) long on the panel line.

(i) Measure up from the floor to mark hem level.

(j) Completed pattern.

Flared skirt

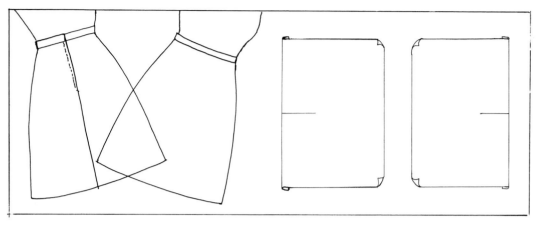

(a) Back and front view of flared skirt.

(b) Cut fabric as for straight skirt, adding 10cm (4") in width on each piece. Mark in the hipline 26.5cm (10½") down from waist.

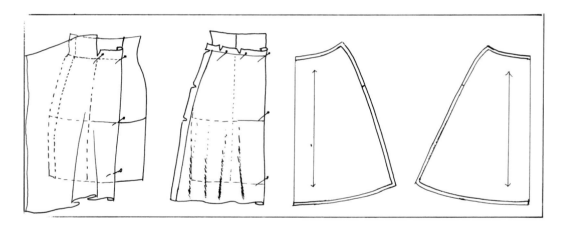

(c) Pin the centre front of fabric to the stand and anchor pin at the top of the stand panel line seam. Allow the fabric to drop towards the centre front at the hemline to increase hem width. Snip to seamline at waist and pin.

(d) Pin side seam and trim surplus fabric. Level hem. Model back in the same way. Mark seams.

(e) Completed pattern.

NEW TECHNIQUES

Omitting the dart and introducing extra hem width

DESIGN NOTE

Flared skirts may be panelled or pleated, fall from a yoke or from a lowered waist. The extra hem width provides the 'walking room'.

Panel line skirt

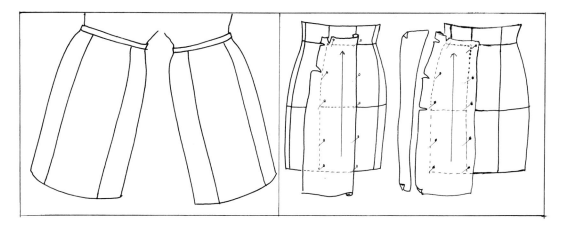

(a) Back and front of the skirt appear the same. The fabric length is divided into four vertical strips. Mark hip level and grainline.

(b) The front skirt is modelled in two pieces: centre front panel and side panel. Model the back panels in the same way.

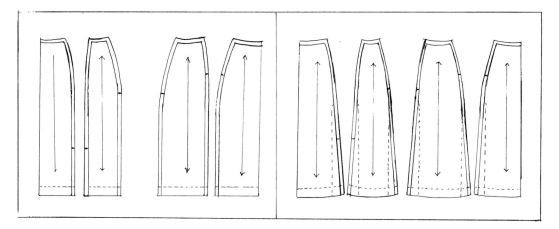

(c) Completed pattern pieces for close-fitting skirt (only suitable for very short skirts).

(d) To add a little flare in longer skirts for a less tapered silhouette and for walking room, increase the hemline at the trueing up stage and run the new seamline into the side seam at hip level.

DESIGN NOTE

This is an elegant skirt for all occasions. The combination of jacket and skirt panel seamlines in a suit or coordinated outfit gives the illusion of height and slenderness.

NEW TECHNIQUES

Adding extra hem width at trueing up stage

Design development

Necklines and their facings

Although neckline facings can be modelled during toile development, it is simpler to draw them on to the toile and trace them off to make a pattern during the trueing up stage.

Modelling with tissue paper
This is a quick and inexpensive way of practising neckline design. Trace off a paper copy of the top 20cm (8") of both left and right sides of a previous block, pin the shoulder seams together and pin to stand. Draw in the full neckline on both sides of the stand, maintaining right angles to centre front and back. After modelling, trace off only the right hand side, to ensure a 'mirror image' when cut double. The new neckline can be traced on to any other block, or separate blocks traced off, each with a different neckline, saving the time and effort of modelling a whole block simply to change the neckline.

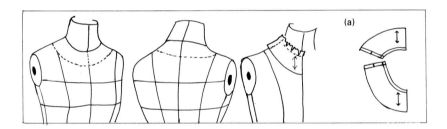

(a) High round necklines need a facing.
Mark 3 points 5cm (2½") from nape, side neck point and front neck. Join these points in a smooth curve. Completed pattern.

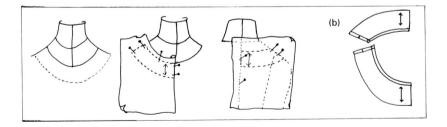

(b) For a lower round neckline, mark the new position in a smooth curve, maintaining right angles at centre front and centre back. Construct the facing 5cm (2½") from this line. Completed pattern.

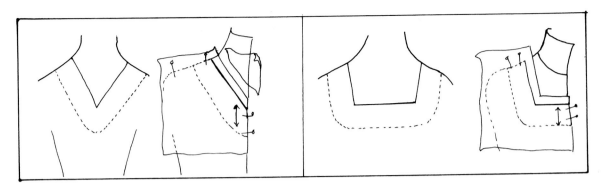

(a) VEE NECKLINE: Tape the new neckline for front and back, and the outer facing edge with a curve at the centre front fold.

(b) SQUARE NECKLINE: Model the 'square' 1.5cm (½") towards centre front at the lower edge.

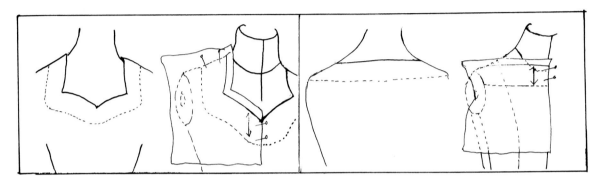

(c) SWEETHEART NECKLINE: Curve the outer edges of the facing.

(d) BATEAU NECKLINE: This is a straight neckline which crosses the neck from a narrow shoulder seam. The facing is stitched into the armhole seam.

NEW TECHNIQUES

Taping the new neckline shape directly on to the stand
Taping the new neckline shape over an otherwise completed toile
Using a paper copy of a previously modelled toile
Creating suitable facings for new necklines

DESIGN NOTE

Neckline shapes are influenced by fashion, fabric, and garment style and function. Whatever their shape, necklines more than 12.5cm (5") below the front neck point are classified as 'low' and require tightening to prevent gaping.

Low necklines

When the front neck point is lowered by more than 12.5cm (5"), the new neckline needs to be tightened to avoid gaping.

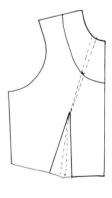

(a) Cut open an existing dart and widen it to accommodate the amount taken in at the neckline. The garment will no longer fit on the stand but will fit closer to the body when worn.

(b) An alternative tightening method is to take the same amount from the centre neckline and run the new centre front fold to the waist. Re-draw grainline.

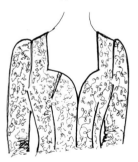

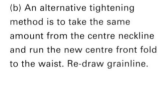

NEW TECHNIQUES

Taping a variety of lowered front and back necklines
Tightening the neckline after modelling

The sketches on this page show various front necklines. All need tightening after modelling. This is done by taking out a dart from the bust point towards the original front neckline or by tightening the seams. The dart position is shown on each sketch. The amount can be determined at the fitting stage. but for average sizes, the dart width would be 1cm (⅜") wide at the stand neckline, therefore about 0.5cm (¼") at the new neckline. If you create even a small dart, the fabric or paper will no longer lie flat. Make these alterations at the trueing up stage.

Widening the neckline reduces the shoulder seam length, and this is often further shortened at the armhole end producing a strap effect. However narrow it is, the shoulder seam will still support the garment, but a boned foundation bodice is needed to keep the garment in place for off-the-shoulder and strapless styles, as shown above.

Front and back necklines do not have to be the same. A low front neckline may need the support of a higher back neckline to stay on the shoulders and vice versa. Where both are low the fit must be very snug and may require elastic or wire support in the seam.

DESIGN NOTE

Most dress stands are too smoothly contoured in the bust area to allow the closer fit required for modelling a low neckline, and a swimwear or lingerie stand may not fulfil the requirements of a designer of party and eveningwear. Special stands can be ordered to accommodate specific needs. This is preferable to adjusting the pattern after modelling because the garment will no longer fit back on to the same stand for evaluation.

Cowl necklines

FRONT BODICE WITH A COWL NECKLINE

Front cowl

(a) Take a square of fabric and stretch it gently from opposite corners against the straight grain.

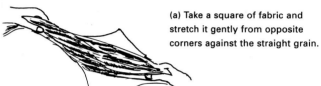

(b) When the fabric is relaxed it falls into deep folds. This is the principle on which cowl drapery is based. The effect of the technique can be compared to folding a square scarf in half diagonally and tying it round the neck which always looks softer than a straight grain scarf.

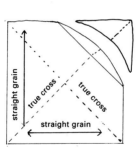

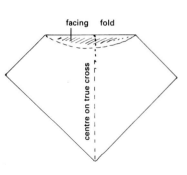

(c) Tape the neckline on the stand.

(d) Cut a length of fabric and square it off. Mark the true cross in both directions. Fold over one corner so as not to show the wrong side of the fabric. The fold must be at least the length of the front neckline plus 5cm (2″). Leave 5cm (2″) for a facing and cut off the remainder.

(e) Gently crease the folded edge and find the centre.

NEW TECHNIQUES

Draping folds across both sides of the stand
Handling fabric on the cross

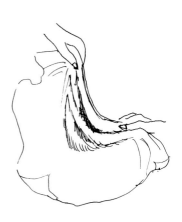 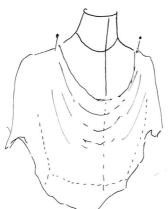 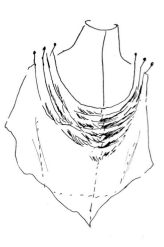

(f) Curl the folded edge from the centre to give it a little 'spring'.

(g) Position the centre of the fabric against the centre stand neckline and pin the fold edge at the shoulders. Check that both sides of the neck are of the same length. Arrange the first folds at centre front.

(h) Keeping the true cross marking in line with the centre front, form pleats either side of the neckline, allowing the folds to fall naturally. Pin.

(i) When satisfied with the neck folds, model the remainder of the bodice, snipping up to the waistline and cutting away surplus fabric. No darts are necessary. The bias cut allows the surplus fabric to be smoothed out into the seamlines.

(j) Mark seamlines and the position of the pleats at the shoulder. Remove from stand and true up.

DESIGN NOTE

The cowl neckline is a classic design used for elegant eveningwear and is equally effective at back or front neck. Although it is possible to use the straight grain of the fabric, the folds form best when cut on the true cross.

Asymmetric styling

In most garments right and left sides are identical, that is, they are a mirror image of each other. In asymmetric designs, one side of the garment looks significantly different to the other and it is necessary to model left and right sides simultaneously. The pieces are cut from single layers of fabric. The back is usually symmetric and is modelled only on one side of the stand.

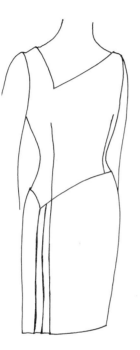

(a) Tape the new neckline and dropped waistline on the stand.
(b) Cut a rectangle of fabric and mark the straight grain and the bustline. Pin fabric to key points as shown. Cut down to neck, up to waist and in to side seams. Form darts, cut away surplus fabric and pin seamlines.
(c) Reduce seam allowance to 1.5cm (½") and mark seamlines and darts.

(a)   (b)   (c)

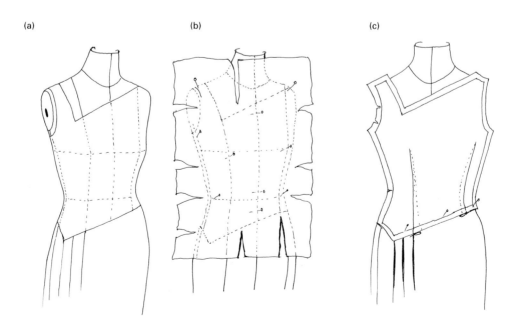

The facings of asymmetric garments must obviously follow the new design edge, except for a back neck facing which can usually be 'placed to fold'.

DESIGN NOTE

Asymmetric styling tends to be used in the more exclusive and, therefore, more expensive garment ranges. It lends itself particularly well to draped styling where the folds can span both sides of the body and be secured by a seam or motif. It is also very effective for smart fitted dresses which fasten away from the more conventional centre front.

Openings

Basic bodice blocks have high, round necklines which encircle the base of the neck.
An opening is usually placed at centre front or centre back of a garment and allows
it to go over the head. Short, faced openings are sometimes used but most openings
extend the full length of the garment.

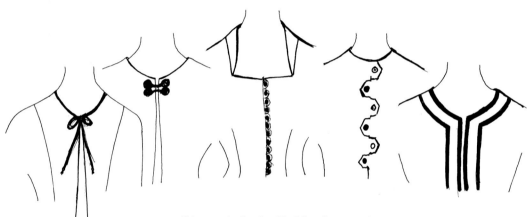

'Edge-to-edge' styles: Model to the centre front or
back. Face or bind the entire outer edge.

Laced bodice: Tape a new front edge short of the
centre front stand seam and model to this line. The
edges of the bodice may be linked by lacing but
cannot meet. Model an all-in-one facing to include
the armhole in sleeveless styles.

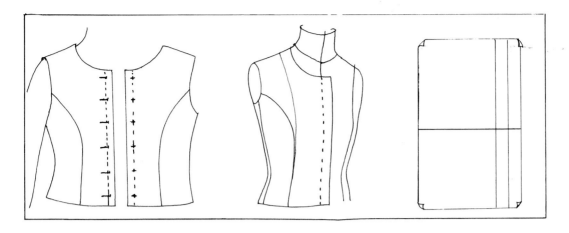

(a) Front jacket

(b) Tape neckline and buttonstand position on the stand.

(c) Allow extra width for the buttonstand on the fabric. Mark the position of bustline, centre front and buttonstand.

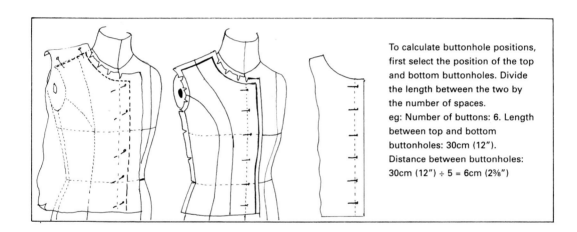

To calculate buttonhole positions, first select the position of the top and bottom buttonholes. Divide the length between the two by the number of spaces.
eg: Number of buttons: 6. Length between top and bottom buttonholes: 30cm (12").
Distance between buttonholes: 30cm (12") ÷ 5 = 6cm (2⅜")

(d) Pin the fabric to the stand, aligning centre front, buttonstand and bustline. Model the new neckline.

(e) Model facing or mark and trace a facing from the completed pattern.

NEW TECHNIQUES

Adding a buttonstand to accommodate buttons and buttonholes
Calculating buttonhole positions

For a centre front opening with buttons, both sides of the garment are identical. Buttons sit exactly on the centre line on the left hand side bodice. On the right hand side, vertical buttonholes are also positioned exactly at the centre but are only used on less fitted garments. Horizontal buttonholes overlap the centre front line very slightly to accommodate the button shank. A centre back opening closes 'left over right'. The button width must be at least the diameter of the button.

Collars

Collars fall into two categories: they either stand above or fall below the normal neckline.

They may be made separately and joined to the garment, be modelled in one with it or be detachable.

Mandarin collar

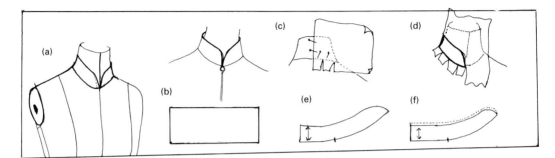

(a) Retape the neckline 1.5cm (½") lower at the centre front.
(b) Cut a rectangle of fabric: ½ neck circumference + 5cm (2") x 4 times the collar's finished height.
(c) Pin fabric to centre back above neckline. Snip to neckline seamline to allow fabric to spread round the neck. Continue round the neck,

keeping the upper edge in line with the tape.
(d) Cut surplus fabric down to 1.5cm (½").
Shape the front neck, mark seams and remove the collar from the stand.
(e) Undercollar.
(f) The top collar has 2mm added to design edge only.

Peter Pan collar

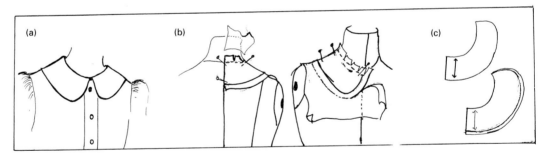

(a) Lower the centre front neckpoint and tape the outer design edge on the stand.

(b) Cut a rectangle of fabric about 2½ times the finished width of the collar. Pin to centre back stand with the surplus above the neckline. Snip fabric to 1.5cm (½") above the nape, then down to neckline. Continue round to centre front. Cut surplus fabric down to 1.5cm (½"). Notch the side neckpoint and mark seamlines and design edge.

(c) Undercollar and top collar with increased design edge.

DESIGN NOTE

Collars provide a finish for the neckline and a frame to enhance the neck and face.
The designer's skill lies in cutting to exactly the right size and shape for the prevailing fashion.

NEW TECHNIQUES

Modelling above the neckline
Modelling from centre back to centre front in one piece

Bertha collar

This collar appears to be asymmetrical because it extends well beyond the centre front of the stand but the two sides are exactly the same.

(a) Double breasted dress with large collar

(b) Attach a padded arm to the stand. Tape a lower neckline to extend beyond the centre front. The design edge encompasses the arm.

(c) Cut a large rectangle of fabric about 46cm (18") square. Model as for the Peter Pan collar as far as the new neck point, then sweep the fabric across the stand, following the new neckline. Complete as for previous collars.

DESIGN NOTE

The Bertha collar is like a small cape. It can be modelled in one with the bodice but is often constructed separately as a contrast collar for smart business wear. Its most popular form is as a pure white collar on a black dress, reminiscent of the Puritan garb of the early American settlers.

NEW TECHNIQUES

Using the padded arm to increase shoulder size
Extending the collar beyond the centre front

Sleeves

This section concentrates on three types of sleeve: sleeves set into the normal bodice armhole, the cap sleeve, and the dropped shoulder, which requires the sleeve head to be reduced.

Straight sleeve

This sleeve falls straight from the under-arm line. It has no dart or ease to shape the elbow. This is the easiest sleeve to model and gives practice in handling the padded arm and managing the sleeve head which has to be eased at the cap to fit the bodice armhole.

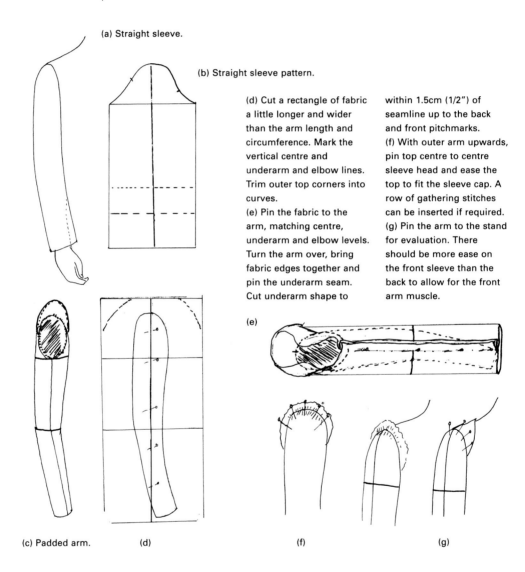

(a) Straight sleeve.

(b) Straight sleeve pattern.

(d) Cut a rectangle of fabric a little longer and wider than the arm length and circumference. Mark the vertical centre and underarm and elbow lines. Trim outer top corners into curves.

(e) Pin the fabric to the arm, matching centre, underarm and elbow levels. Turn the arm over, bring fabric edges together and pin the underarm seam. Cut underarm shape to within 1.5cm (1/2") of seamline up to the back and front pitchmarks.

(f) With outer arm upwards, pin top centre to centre sleeve head and ease the top to fit the sleeve cap. A row of gathering stitches can be inserted if required.

(g) Pin the arm to the stand for evaluation. There should be more ease on the front sleeve than the back to allow for the front arm muscle.

(e)

(c) Padded arm.　　　(d)　　　　　　　　(f)　　　　　　　　(g)

NEW TECHNIQUES

Using the padded arm both independently and when attached to the stand
Easing surplus fabric at the sleeve head

Fitted sleeve

Fitted sleeves narrow slightly from underarm to elbow, then more obviously from elbow to wrist, following the natural forward slant of the arm. When narrower than about 23cm (9") they require an opening on the back line.

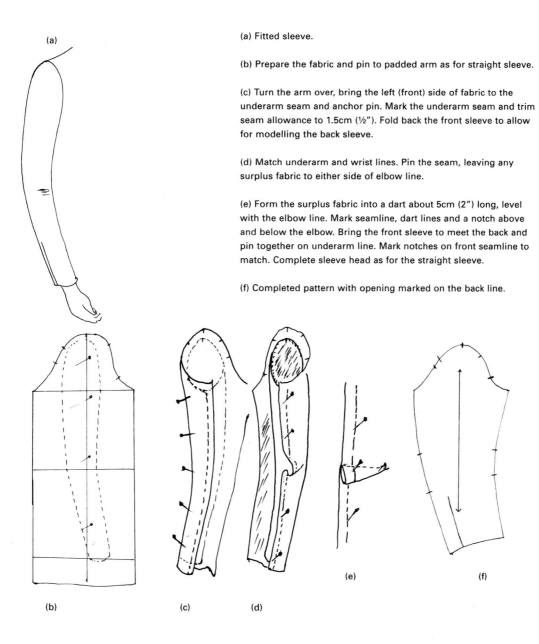

(a) Fitted sleeve.

(b) Prepare the fabric and pin to padded arm as for straight sleeve.

(c) Turn the arm over, bring the left (front) side of fabric to the underarm seam and anchor pin. Mark the underarm seam and trim seam allowance to 1.5cm (½"). Fold back the front sleeve to allow for modelling the back sleeve.

(d) Match underarm and wrist lines. Pin the seam, leaving any surplus fabric to either side of elbow line.

(e) Form the surplus fabric into a dart about 5cm (2") long, level with the elbow line. Mark seamline, dart lines and a notch above and below the elbow. Bring the front sleeve to meet the back and pin together on underarm line. Mark notches on front seamline to match. Complete sleeve head as for the straight sleeve.

(f) Completed pattern with opening marked on the back line.

Short sleeves

For short sleeves, adapt straight or fitted sleeve blocks to save re-modelling.

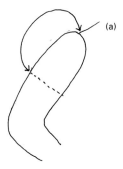

(a)

(a) Puff sleeve: to determine the extra fabric required for a puff sleeve, measure an imaginary 'puff' on the padded arm.

(b) Puff sleeve.

(c) Shorten the straight sleeve pattern.

d) Slash the pattern and spread out on fabric. Lengthen top and lower edges. Cut out the new pattern shape and gather top and lower edges.

(e) Adjust the gathers on the padded arm to fit armhole and top arm.

(b)

(c)

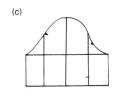

(d)

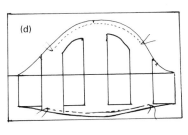

(e)

(a)

(b)

(c)

(a) Short sleeve with gathered top.

(b) Shorten the fitted sleeve pattern, slash on the centre line and open top as shown. Pin pattern to fabric and draw on the extra height and width required. Straighten lower edge.

(c) Gather the sleeve head and adjust the armhole to fit on the padded arm.

A variety of gathered sleeves.

Long sleeves

TWO-PIECE LEG O' MUTTON SLEEVE

Copy the fitted sleeve pattern on to paper and divide as shown. Make the upper part as a puff and the lower part as a fitted sleeve with wrist opening. Check fit and appearance on the padded arm.

ONE-PIECE LEG O' MUTTON SLEEVE

Use the fitted sleeve block as a guide. Draw the new width and height directly on to the fabric. Complete the sleeve on the padded arm.

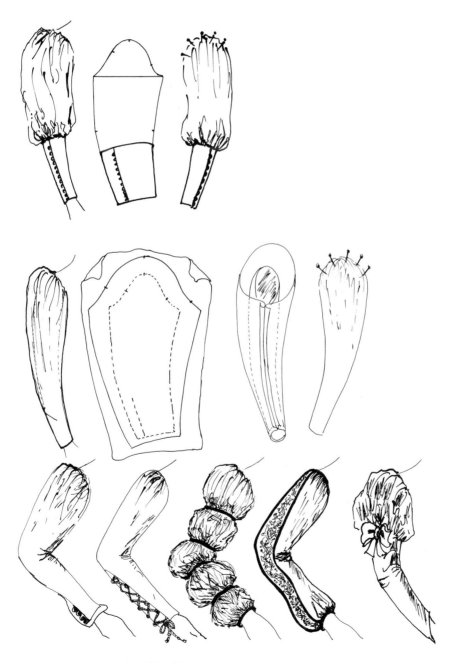

A variety of long sleeves.

For cap sleeve and dropped shoulder styles, the arm needs to be attached to the stand. Use a shoulder pad covered with card to raise the shoulder.

Cap sleeve

For the cap sleeve, mark the extended shoulder seam and rejoin it to the side seam 2cm (¾") below the normal underarm point to increase the armhole length.

Dropped shoulder

Dropped shoulder styles may or may not include a sleeve. Adjust as for sleeveless style (pp26-7). Remove sleeve cap for all sleeve styles.

Sleeve for new armhole

Model the small sections to be removed from outlined sleeve block.

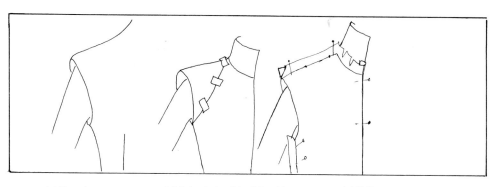

(a) Cap sleeve.   (b) Raised shoulder (shoulder pad covered with card).   (c) Toile.

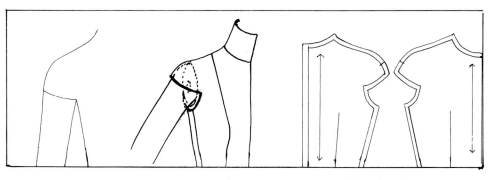

(d) Dropped shoulder.   (e) Taped dropped shoulder and lower armhole.   (f) Completed bodice pattern.

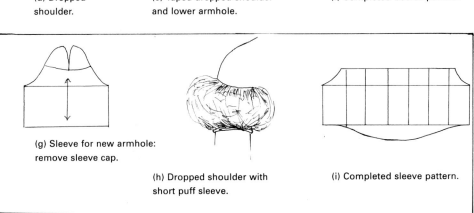

(g) Sleeve for new armhole: remove sleeve cap.

(h) Dropped shoulder with short puff sleeve.

(i) Completed sleeve pattern.

Separate sleeves

DESIGN NOTE

Separate sleeves are worn with evening, party and dancewear, with sleeveless styles and when the garment has no shaped armhole, as with some strapless styles. The sleeve head is cut off completely from the underarm upwards. The sleeve length may be increased to reach almost up to the shoulder or down to the fingers. Use the fitted sleeve block for fitted styles, and for gathered sleeves, adapt the straight sleeve block. This page shows a selection of separate sleeves.

Skirt styling

Yoked skirt

Tape the yokeline on the stand. Pin the straight grain of fabric to centre front of stand. Smooth fabric to the side seam, snipping to the waist seamline. This skirt has no dart. The lower part of the skirt may be in any style, plus buttonstand.

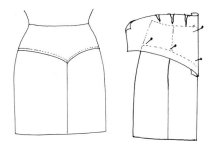

Button-through hipster skirt and belt

Tape a lower waistline on the stand. Model right half only to the buttonstand edge and include the lower end of the dart. Model a facing for top edge and buttonstand.

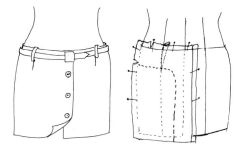

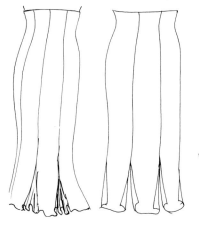

Raised waist panel line with godet

Tape a raised waistline on to the stand bodice. Model as for longer version of panel line skirt block but leave the seam ends open.

A godet is a triangular piece of fabric inserted in the skirt to increase the hemline and so provide walking room. To make the godet, construct a semi-circle, the radius of which should be the length of the opening.

Handkerchief skirt

The handkerchief skirt is modelled from squares of fabric joined on the straight grain, the true cross falling from waist to points. Four squares will give a four-pointed skirt. One corner is cut off to make room for the waist (cut off corner = ¼ waist measurement). The more squares there are, the smaller the cut corner need be. Experiment with layers of squares in fine fabrics.

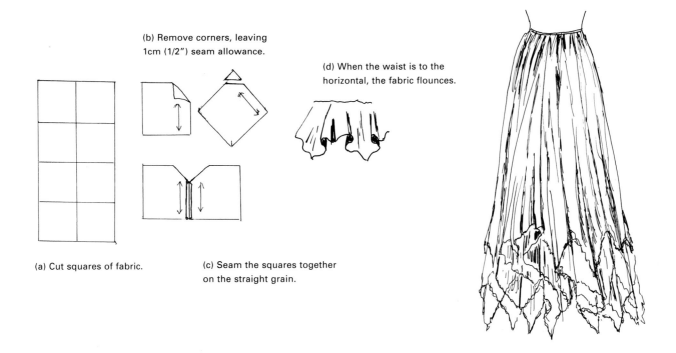

(b) Remove corners, leaving 1cm (1/2″) seam allowance.

(d) When the waist is to the horizontal, the fabric flounces.

(a) Cut squares of fabric.

(c) Seam the squares together on the straight grain.

Skirt fully gathered on to yoke

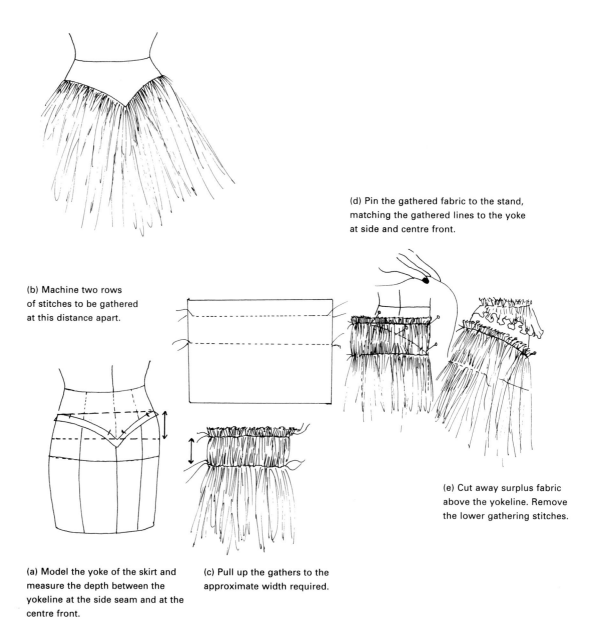

56

(b) Machine two rows of stitches to be gathered at this distance apart.

(d) Pin the gathered fabric to the stand, matching the gathered lines to the yoke at side and centre front.

(e) Cut away surplus fabric above the yokeline. Remove the lower gathering stitches.

(a) Model the yoke of the skirt and measure the depth between the yokeline at the side seam and at the centre front.

(c) Pull up the gathers to the approximate width required.

DESIGN NOTE

Fully gathered skirts set on lowered waistlines emphasize narrow waists and the wide hems add to the illusion. Such skirts are very popular for party, dancing and bridalwear.

NEW TECHNIQUES

Modelling pre-gathered fabric to a shaped seamline

Gathered fishtail skirt

A gathered fishtail for a dress or skirt uses the same principle as the gathered skirt with a yoke seam. Allow extra width if a train is included, as in the example below.

If a flounced fishtail is required, that is, with no gathers, smooth the fabric at the seam edge and work on the principle of circular cutting (see p59). This technique is suitable for heavier fabrics which may be too bulky if gathered.

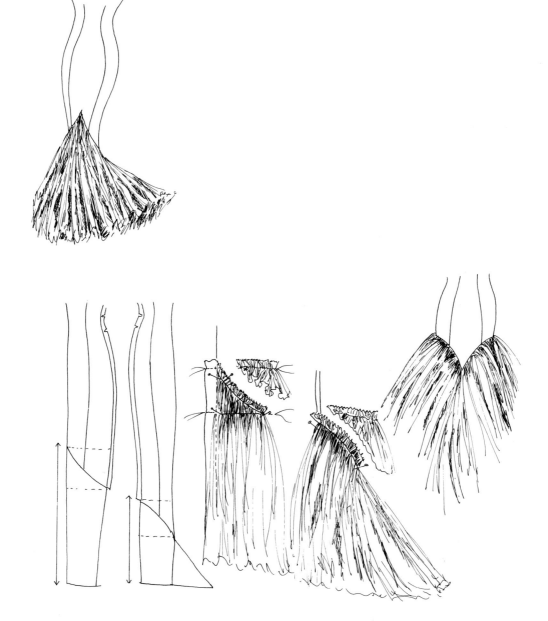

Frills and flounces

Frills

Frills add femininity to skirts, necklines and sleeves. Allow 3-4 times the original fabric measurement for fine fabrics, less than this for thicker fabrics.

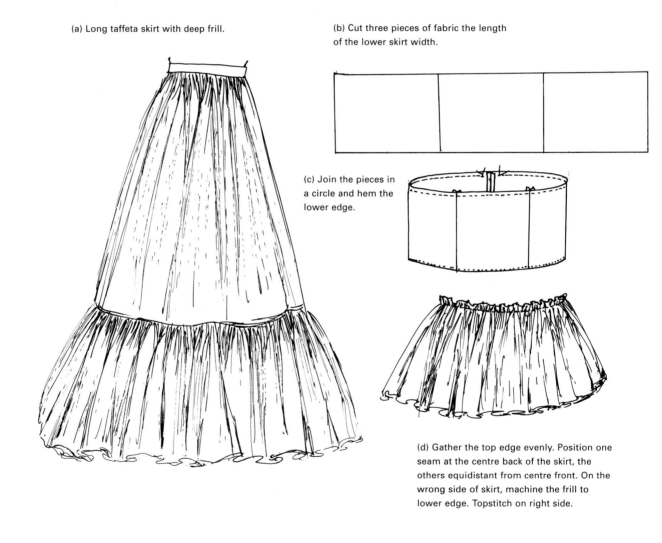

(a) Long taffeta skirt with deep frill.

(b) Cut three pieces of fabric the length of the lower skirt width.

(c) Join the pieces in a circle and hem the lower edge.

(d) Gather the top edge evenly. Position one seam at the centre back of the skirt, the others equidistant from centre front. On the wrong side of skirt, machine the frill to lower edge. Topstitch on right side.

Flounces and circular cutting techniques

Flounces resemble frills but are wider at the hem edge. The top edge, which is seamed to the garment, may be smooth or gathered. Flounces are very effective on necklines and sleeve ends and the same principle can be used for adding fullness to a lower skirt, for instance, as an alternative to the gathered fishtail.

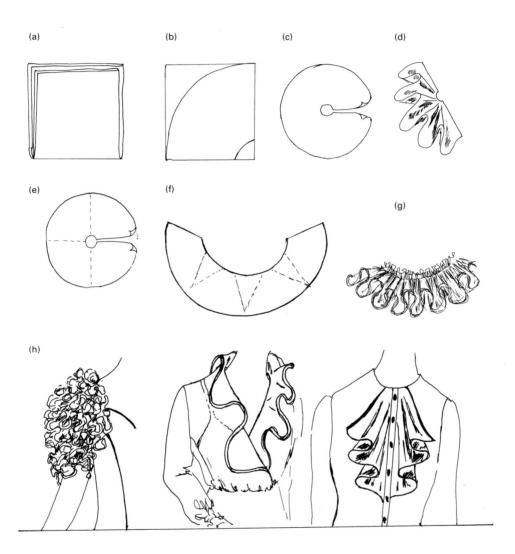

(a) Fold a square of fabric twice.
(b) Draw two quarter circles, one at the folded corner for the centre and the second for the outer circle.
(c) Cut along one fold to open the circle.
(d) One circular flounce. Join any number of flounces to make the length required.

(e) For gathered flounces, prepare a paper circle, slash to outer edge and spread out to increase upper edge.
(f) Cut the required amount of flounces from this shape.
(g) Gather along the upper edge.
(h) Use flounces to enhance necklines and sleeves.

Advanced modelling

Strapless blocks

The strapless blocks in this section follow classic lines favoured by designers of clothes for special occasions. When made up in different fabrics they are suitable for most climates and for evening or daywear. The blocks may be modelled to the waist or to any level below this, and be shaped at the top or lower edges to achieve various designs. The upper edge of the block and the area immediately under the bust need a tighter fit than the normal stand allows. This tightening can be done during the trueing stage. Once tightened, the toile will no longer fit on the stand, so it is wise to keep a copy of the original, unaltered, to use as a foundation for other advanced styles. This tightening is essential if the block is to be used without further styling, as in the sketches below.

Blocks with no armhole; only suitable for a separate sleeve

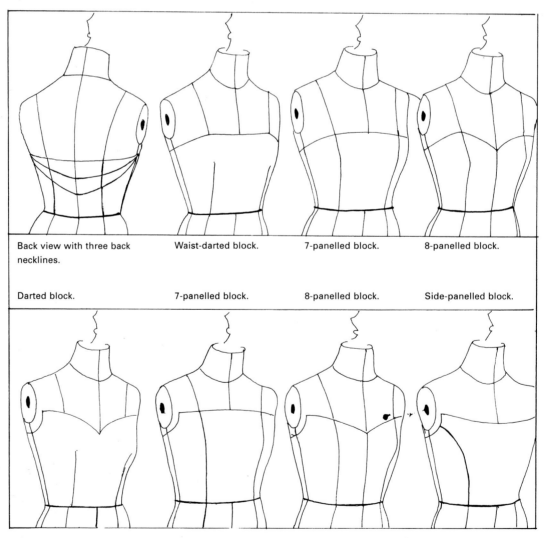

Back view with three back necklines.

Waist-darted block.

7-panelled block.

8-panelled block.

Darted block.

7-panelled block.

8-panelled block.

Side-panelled block.

Blocks with half an armhole; suitable for half armhole sleeves and shoulder drapes

Many designers use a set of strapless blocks as patterns without further adaptation. The variety in their collections is achieved through clever choice of different fabrics, colours, trimmings and accessories.

The term 'strapless' means that the bodice is not supported by shoulder seams or straps and so requires other means to stay in place, usually boning (see p66).

Shoulders carry the weight of a garment and even narrow shoulder seams will render a boned support unnecessary. Where straps are the only support, a bra is usually worn to retain the bodice shape. Straps are often used as a decorative rather than a functional aspect of design and boned bodices stay in place with or without them.

This section presents the three strapless blocks which form the basis of all strapless styles: darted, 7- or 8-panel and side panel lines. Variation is introduced by changing the shape of the upper edge, that is, the neckline, and the waistline, which may be of differing styles or lowered to such an extent that the bodice becomes a dress. The shortened skirt may become a frill, flounce or fishtail, or disappear altogether. Page 69 gives further ideas on neckline design and dropped waistlines.

62

Darted bodice block

Instructions are given here for darts at both back and front. A low back, however, holds its shape better with a panel line. Model on the right hand side of stand only, but it helps visually if the the left hand side of the stand is taped.

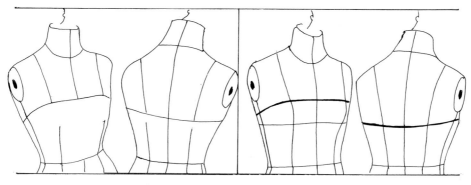

(a) Front, back.

(b) Tape the front bodice upper edge, sloping under the armhole and straightening out across centre back.

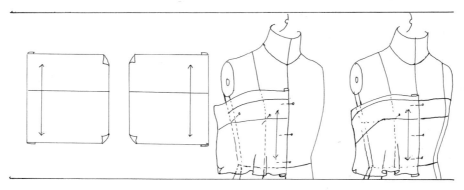

(c) Cut a piece of fabric, the length of the distance of the upper bodice over the bust point to the waist, plus 5cm (2"). Mark the bust level. Divide lengthwise into two strips and mark the straight grain. Fold under 2cm (1") on outer edges.

(d) Pin the fabric to the stand, matching centre front and bustline. Anchor pin bust point.

(e) Smooth fabric above the bustline towards side. Hold the fabric at the underarm and let the surplus fall below the bust point.

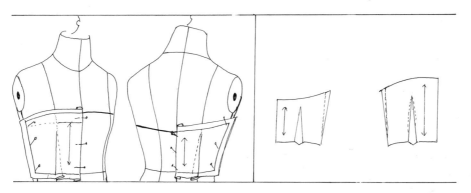

(f) Pin side seam. Snip lower fabric up to waistline. Pin a dart, finishing short of the bust point, turned towards the centre front.

(g) Model the back bodice in the same way.

(h) Tighten side seam and dart as shown before adding seam allowance.

Shoulder panel line bodice block

This block is constructed of 8 panels, or 7, if the centre front or back is cut on the fold.
These diagrams show the modelling of the 7-panel block.

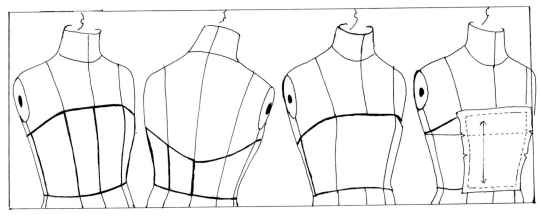

(a) Stand taped for 8-panel block plus upper edge.

(b) Front stand taped for 7-panel block.

(c) Model across the bust cleavage for a close fit.

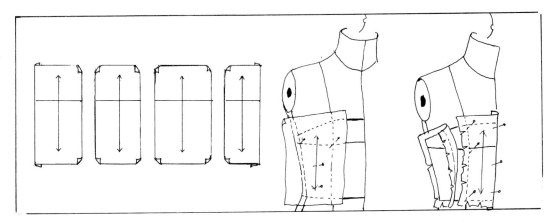

(d) Prepare fabric strips to fit the panels.

(e) Model the side front panel.

(f) Fold back the side panel and model the centre panel. For a 7-panel block, model between bust points.

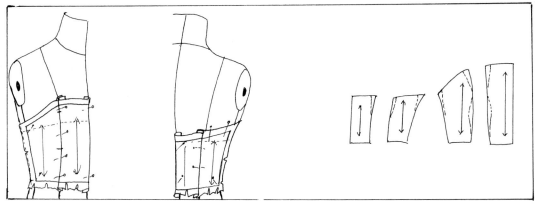

(g) Complete the front panel seam.

(h) Model the back panels.

(i) True the pattern and tighten as shown before adding the seam allowance.

Side panel line bodice block

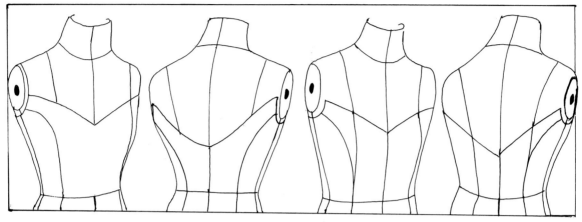

(a) Side panel bodice with half armhole.

(b) Tape the side panel line on the stand.

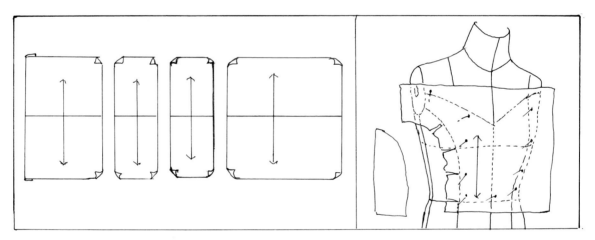

(c) Prepare fabric sections. The front piece spans the whole front of the stand. Mark bust level and straight grain. Fold 2cm (¾") under for centre back.

(d) Model the centre front panel to the curved panel line.

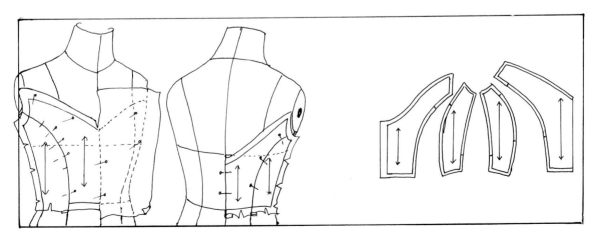

(e) Cut neckline. Model the side panel and complete panel seam.

(f) Model the back panels following the new panel line.

(g) Remove from stand, true up and tighten below the bust and the the top of the seams as for the side panel block. Add seam allowance.

Boned foundation bodice block

Boning may be bought wholesale and cut as needed, in which case the sharp ends must be covered to avoid penetrating the garment fabric and causing physical discomfort to the wearer.

Professional dressmakers and manufacturers of strapless garments order pre-cut and finished bones requiring no extra preparation.

Three types of boning are in common use.

(a) Spiral boning (2 wires in a continuous coil) which bends forwards, backwards and sideways and is durable and washable. Use where the body needs to bend.

(b) Stiff plastic, which has taken the place of whalebone which is more rigid. Use in the back bodice and side seams. Both these types must be inserted into a casing.

(c) 'Rigilene', a 'boning' made of 8 nylon filaments woven into a continuous strip, is a substitute for whalebone but is not as strong. However, it can be machined along its vertical edges straight on to the fabric and does not require a casing.

A boned foundation is a separate layer of a strapless bodice which may also be used as the bodice lining. In high-quality garments the boned layer is inserted between the outer and the lining layers. The foundation shapes the bodice and prevents it slipping down the body. The outer bodice design can be cut to different design lines and is stitched to the shaped foundation for support.

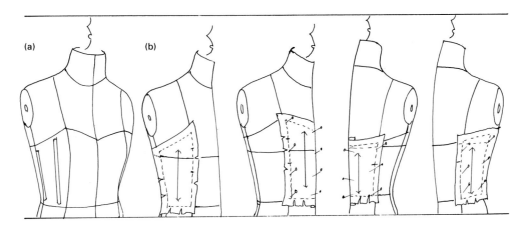

(a) Tape upper and lower foundation bodice design lines on the stand. These will be identical to those of the outer and lining layers.

(b) Model the four panels.

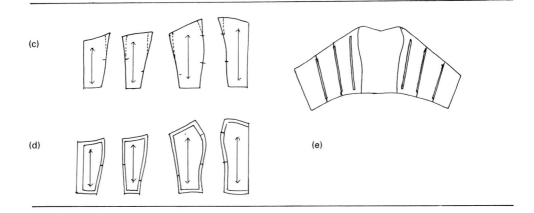

(c) Remove from the stand, true lines and make a paper or card pattern without tightening for future use. Whenever a foundation needs to be cut in fabric for another strapless style, it will be tightened with the garment.

(d) To tighten the bodice to fit the body closely, mark new seamlines above and below the bust and on other seams as shown.

(e) Made-up foundation bodice showing boning positions: side seams, back panel lines, and away from the front panel line, producing a more subtle shape than if taken directly over the bust.

Hip-length strapless block

Darts or panel lines which extend below the waistline in strapless blocks are modelled in the same way as the basic hip block on page 28. Choose an appropriate lower edge for the block. The lower edge of the block may be any shape, but if joined to a skirt section, the top edge of the skirt must follow the same line.

Bustiers

Bustiers, derived from a foundation garment, can be worn for day and eveningwear either as a bodice or over a bodice and skirt. Traditionally boned and fastened with lacing, they can now feature zips or buttons and can be made in anything from velvet to denim. The bustiers featured here only need very small pieces of fabric to follow the curves of the bust.

Tape the stand following the seamlines on the bustier design. Use small scraps of fabric. Measure the length and width of each tiny section and add a small amount to each side for handling. Model the sections in any order. Follow the taped outlines precisely to achieve the crisp finish which is a feature of this type of garment.

Ideas for necklines and waistlines with strapless designs.

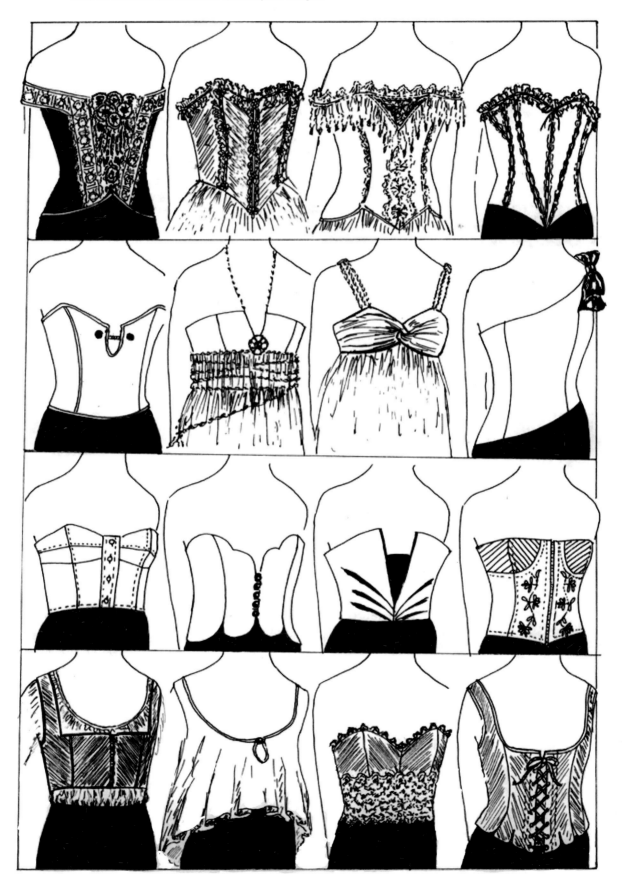

Ruching

The principles of ruching

Consider the fabric, whether it is fine or
heavy, plain or patterned.
Decide how dense the gathers should be.
Estimate the fabric width and length for the
ruched area.
Consider if the ruching needs to be supported
before insertion.
Decide how it is to be sewn into the garment.

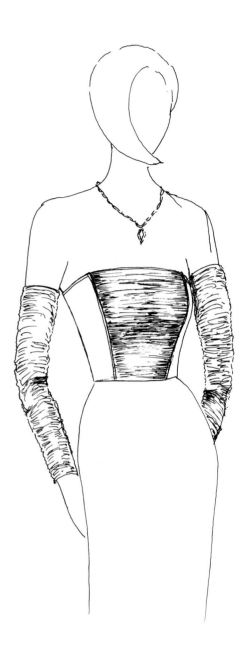

DESIGN NOTE

Ruching or quilling is the term given to gathering fabric into
small, cylindrical folds resembling reeds or quills. The ruched
areas are controlled by seams. In narrow panels, the folds
remain consistently spaced and closely packed, but a centre
front panel which spans the bust curve forces the gathers apart,
slightly flattening them. Visuallly, ruching has the effect of
increasing the size of the wearer and is flattering to the most
slender figures.

NEW TECHNIQUES

Estimating fabric quantities for ruching
Concealment of fabric joins within ruched areas
Modelling over a prepared foundation

When cutting the fabric, allow 3 times the amount needed for the finished length. Use a set square to find the true cross (at a 45 degree angle to the straight grain). Mark off the required number of pieces. Mark notches for joining and the straight grain on each. Mark the wrong side of the fabric so that the pieces can be matched together correctly. Make narrow seams and press them all in the same direction.

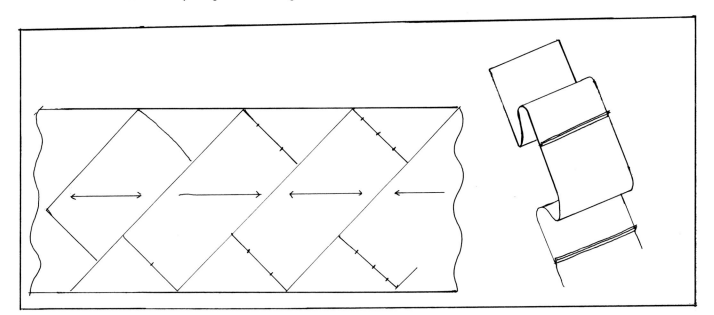

DESIGN NOTE

Ruching is most effective when cut on the true cross of the fabric which is very flexible and stretches widthwise. Note that joins on the cross are not seamed on the straight grain or else the seam would show up as a diagonal line, as on piping.

Ruched central panel

The ruched panel is gathered separately then modelled over a backing panel which supports the gathers. The two layers are then seamed to the side front panels before joining to the back bodice. The whole bodice is stitched to a boned foundation.

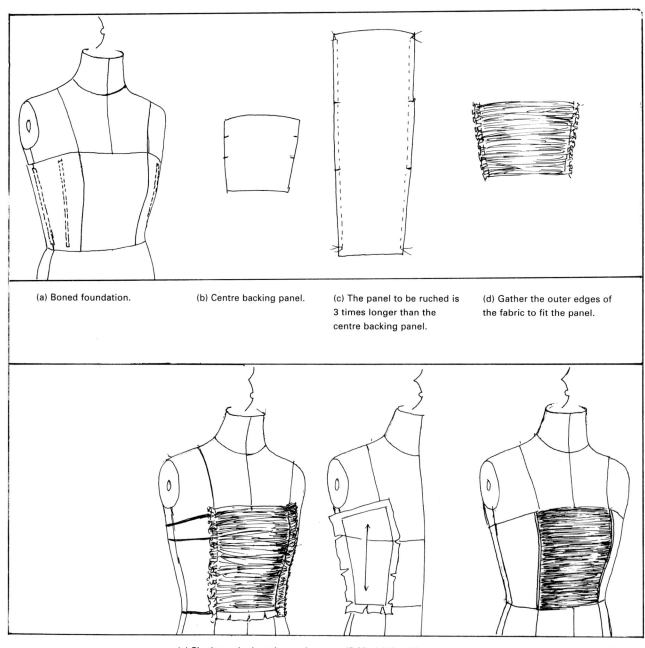

(a) Boned foundation.

(b) Centre backing panel.

(c) The panel to be ruched is 3 times longer than the centre backing panel.

(d) Gather the outer edges of the fabric to fit the panel.

(e) Pin the ruched section to the stand, adjust gathers and pin to backing panel on panel lines. Remove the two layers from the stand and tack outer edges. Randomly stitch between the folds.

(f) Model the side panel.

(g) Join to side panels and complete the bodice.

Hip-length ruched bodice cut on the cross

This bodice has side seams, and has either a side zip to the underarm or a centre back opening with button and loop or zip fastening.

Although fabric cut on the cross can be lengthened by seaming together two pieces with the join hidden between the folds, it is not wise to add width in this way because the seam will be visible diagonally and interrupt the folds.

The bodice can be made with the ruching on the diagonal. The fabric may be cut on the straight grain or the cross and the two outer lengthwise edges pulled in opposite directions to distort their symmetry.

Ruched bodices should be modelled over a foundation. After modelling, tighten the ruched section at the side seams.

73

(a) Ruched hip length bodice.

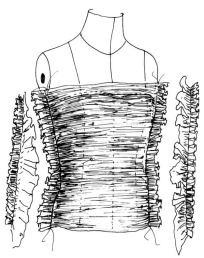

(b) Model the ruched fabric over a foundation.

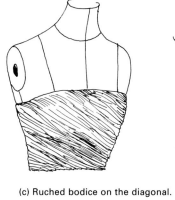

(c) Ruched bodice on the diagonal.

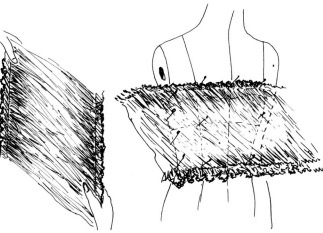

(d) Ruching can be distorted to create diagonal folds.

(e) Modelling the diagonal ruching.

Ruched mini dress and sleeves

Model the lining sections and leave them pinned but un-sewn to the stand.

Cut a piece of fabric 3 times the finished length for front and back dress and two sleeves. The back of the dress will have a centre seam with an opening. Seam the fabric, press, and gather ruched sections to the desired dress and sleeve lengths.

Model and pin the ruched sections over the lining sections. Remove each section from the stand and tack the ruching to the lining. Each dress section now has two layers which will be seamed at sides and centre back. Seam the sleeve underarm and insert sleeve. Complete neck and hems.

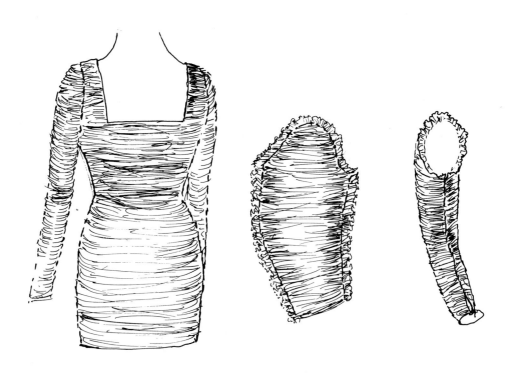

(a) Ruched dress over lining.   (b) Ruched sleeve seams.   (c) Completed sleeve.

The following chart suggests ways of including ruching in dress design. All are based on the blocks shown in this book. Select a block to use as a foundation, cut lengths of bias-cut fabric for ruching and experiment for different effects. If you do not have a particular foundation block available or the design is unusual, tape the stand to the new design, model and complete a pattern for the foundation shape, and then follow the principles of ruching as previously demonstrated.

Stretch fabrics

Stretch fabrics are used for body conforming garments. The degree of stretch (extension) and recovery (return to unstretched state) varies according to the fabric. Dresses and casual tops require far less elasticity than garments worn for sports such as skating, swimming and cycling, where close fit and vigorous action demand a high level of recovery. For such garments choose superstretch fabrics. The stretch factor is found in many types of fabric, from denim to lace and beaded and sequinned materials. Avoid using facings, which add bulk and hem or bind edges using stretch stitches.

A standard dress stand is suitable for modelling tops and dresses in stretch fabrics. Remove any additional padding as this provides necessary tolerance for body movement in woven fabrics. Check body measurements against the stand. If any part of the stand is larger than the corresponding body measurement many designers prefer to use a stand one size smaller.

Mini dress

This long-sleeved mini dress can be used as a block to develop many other dress and T-shirt designs. Make a toile in stretch cotton jersey. Complete the pattern and add cut-off marks for shorter tops. If superstretch fabric is is used, the garment will pull over the head; otherwise make a short opening at the neckline. Most of the following garments start with a high neckline, but various shapes can be added.

Use a stand and an arm adjusted to body measurements. Raise the stand underarm point by 2cm (¾"). Tape a smaller armhole, approximately 35cm (13¾") in circumference, on the stand and arm.

Model the back and front dress simultaneously. Stretch fabrics may be tubular or flat and of various widths. Tubular fabrics have foldmarks where the fabric is flattened when rolled. Use the folds for the garment sides which will be cut to shape the body. If fabric is non-tubular, cut off one dress length and pin the cut edges together to form a tube.

(a) One tubular dress length. Mark centre front, centre back and bustline.

(b) Pull the tube over the stand, matching centres and bustline. Anchor pin shoulders and bust points.

(c) Grasp the fabric at both sides, taking in equal amounts so that the fabric fits the stand from underarm to hem. Pin the side seams.

(d) Shape the neckline and armhole and pin the shoulder seam. The whole fit should be smooth.

(e) Cut a piece of fabric the length of the arm. Mark the centre and underarm line.

(f) Pin the fabric to the arm, matching marked lines.

(g) Turn the arm over and pin the underarm seam.

(h) Smooth fabric over the top of the arm and pin to the smaller armhole. Allow narrow seam allowance. Mark seams and remove from the arm.

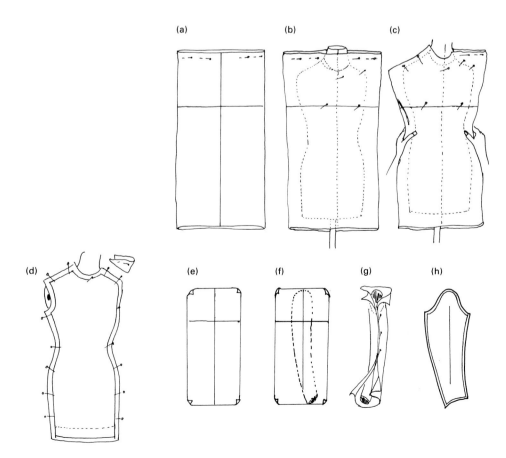

(a) (b) (c)

(d) (e) (f) (g) (h)

Stands with legs

A stand with legs is needed to model nether garments - those with a division between the legs such as unitards, tights, swimwear, shorts and trousers. There are four types of stand available.

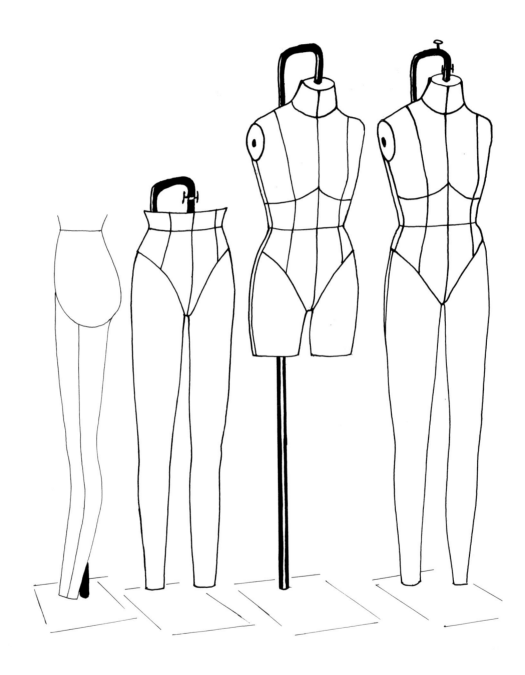

(a) One leg stand: ideal for modelling nether garments with a crotch seam.

(b) Two-leg stand: for garments with or without a crotch seam and swimming costumes.

c) Half length (neck to thigh): excellent for leotards, swimwear and shorts.

(d) Full length (neck to ankle): suitable for all types of garment.

The following pages offer a selection of stretch garments to model, including one and two piece swimsuits and an evening dress.

(a) Unitard (top and legs in one).

(b) Crop top and briefs over unitard.

(d) Leotard over tights.

(c) Crop top and running shorts.

Crop tops and vests

These instructions are for plain garments. Impose your own design lines and experiment with shapes and colours to make combinations of tops and running shorts and tights.

Crop tops and vests are easy to model. Tape the neck and armhole on the stand. Cut a piece of fabric the width of the shoulders by the length of top required. Prepare as for the tube dress and put on the stand. Complete the neck and armholes. Leave the side seams fairly straight for the vest, but shape those of the crop top from the underarm so it fits snugly below the bust in the midriff area.

To make a variety of tops, model toiles in plain, light-coloured, inexpensive material, then draw design lines on to the fabric. The final fabric is modelled over the toile following these new design lines.

Shorts and tights

Use superstretch lycra or nylon with a 2-way stretch for shorts which fit the body like a second skin. Model these styles on a trouser stand. For tights with a centre front and back seam, model half the stand only.

Measure the top of the back leg at the widest part (crotch level) from side seam to inner leg and add 5cm (2"). Cut two pieces of fabric this width by the desired length plus 10cm (4").
Mark crotch level.

For tights, cut the fabric to the length required. Follow the directions given for shorts until the crotchline and top leg are completed, then continue to model the legs, keeping the straight grain level with the centre front and back leg tape.

(a) The crotch seam length is the distance from the front waist to inner leg seam, through to back waist.
(b) Tape the centre, front and back leg, crotch level and hemline.
(c) Pin the fabric to the stand matching crotch level and straight grain to the centre leg.
(d) Smooth fabric out from the centre and pin side seam, inner leg and centre front seam.
(e) Completed front leg.
(f) Taped back stand.
(g) Model the back shorts in the same way.
(h) Stretch the fabric to encompass the seat curve. Mark seams.
(i) Completed pattern.

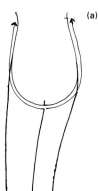

(a)

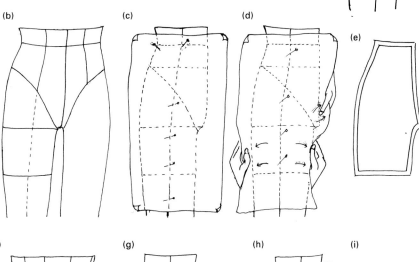

(b) (c) (d) (e)

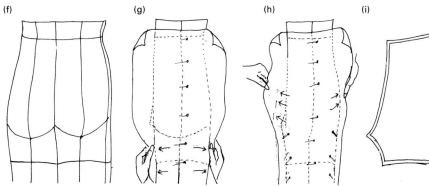

(f) (g) (h) (i)

Seamed unitard

The unitard is a version of the leotard including both bodice and legs. Superstretch fabrics make possible full-length action clothes that stretch to maximum body movement and immediately recover their original shape when still.

Model the unitard with a centre seam at the back and front. The neck and armholes can be variously shaped and the legs of any length.

82

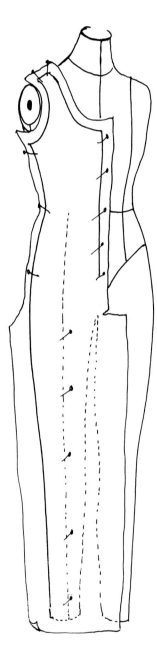

(a) Cut two pieces of fabric, the shoulder to ankle length plus 5cm (2") x 36cm (14"), and pin to the stand as shown. Work on front and back simultaneously. Model down to hip and snip to crotch at the centre front. Shape front and back crotchlines and upper leg as for the shorts. Complete the remainder of leg in the same way as the tights.

(b) Completed pattern.

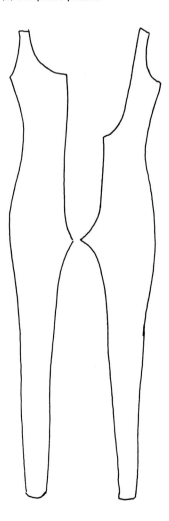

Unitard without centre front seam

Omitting the centre front seam gives scope for interesting design lines. Side panels
and aerodynamic body curves flatter sleek athletic figures. Use elastomeric piping or
contrast stretch stitching to emphasize design lines. The back is seamed to allow for
the long, curved crotch seam which comes further forward when there is no centre
front seam.

(a) Cut a piece of fabric for the front to cover both sides of the stand. The fabric for the back is in two
pieces. Pin the back and front to the stand and complete modelling down to hip level. Cut the front fabric
through centre up to within 2cm (¾″) of the front crotch seam.

(b) Complete the modelling of the front legs. The back is shaped as in previous exercises. Stretch the
fabric well forward to meet the front crotch shaping.

(c) Measure the stand through the crotchline to check the total crotch seam length.

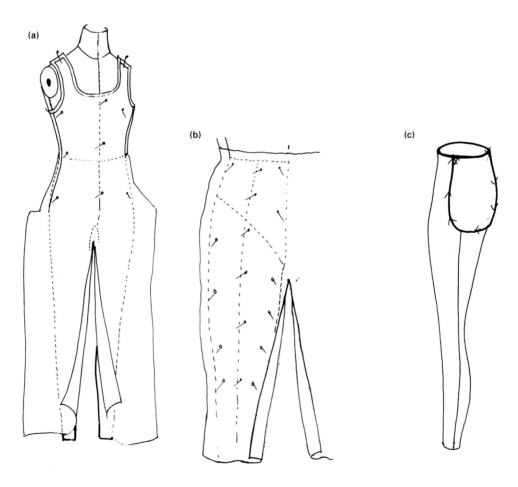

(a)

(b)

(c)

Swimsuits

The revolution in stretch fabrics has produced superstretch materials with 100 per cent recovery. Swimwear can now be modelled as a second skin in sleek, body-fitting styles resistant to chlorine, salt water, sun and mildew. Fewer seams for shaping has led to new design possibilities and the return of the one-piece swimsuit.

Most swimsuit fabrics contain lycra (US: Spandex), a man-made elastic fibre which is woven or knitted with other fibres to produce fabrics which stretch but can recover their original length.

Swimsuits can be cut low on the back and well away from the normal armhole to allow for vigorous movement and can have skin-revealing cut-outs, sleeves and legs. If panels or bands of contrast colours are inserted, make sure all the fabrics have the same elastomeric properties.

84

One-piece swimsuit

A simply shaped swimsuit made from 2 pieces
of fabric can be adapted from the mini dress block.

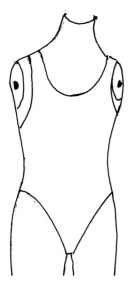

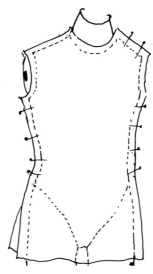

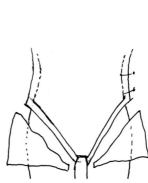

(a) Use a stand with legs.
Tape the desired neckline,
armhole and leg shape.
There is no centre front or
back seam

(b) Model as for the mini
dress to 10cm (4") below
the crotch level, leaving
the side seams open
below high hip level.

(c) Smooth the fabric downwards and pin
to the centre front, following the stand
crotch seam between the legs. Place the
narrow horizontal seam joining the front
and back sections towards the back of the
garment. The crotch width should be of a
minimum of 3cm (1¼") from the stand
centre seamline, giving 6cm (2½") width
in the completed garment.

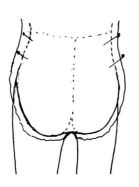

(d) Model the back
crotchline in the same
way and complete the
side seams.

(e) Side view.

(f) Mark the neck and armhole lines and
cut, leaving seam allowance. Model a
lining which closely moulds the bust
contour and insert bra cups. The entire
crotch section is also lined.

Two-piece swimsuit

(a) For the twisted top, cut a piece of fabric 30cm (12") long by 88cm (34") wide. Turn in 2.5cm (1") facings towards the wrong side on the long edges. Finger gather the material and twist the fabric length twice to simulate a knot. Pin to the centre front stand between the bust points and stretch the ends round to the centre back. Gather each end and attach a fastener or join in a tube and gather. Line the top and insert bust cups if wished.

For the bikini briefs, tape a high hipline and leg shape on stand. Model in the same way as the crotch area of the one-piece swimsuit.

(b) For the sectioned bra, model a stretch lining and insert bra cups. Draw the desired design lines on to this plain base. Cut small pieces of swimwear fabric, all of the same type, and model to the drawn design lines.

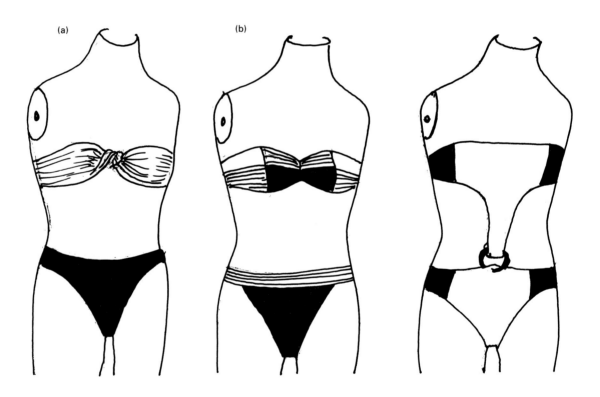

(a)   (b)

DESIGN NOTE

The bra section may be simply a tube of fabric which can be pulled over the head or stepped into. The fit must be very snug.

Evening dress designs

Backless evening dress

Use the stretch mini dress toile pattern, cut to the length required, make up and put on the stand. Tape the new neckline over it, taking it wide of the armhole in the front and sloping down to the back midriff. Straps extend from the high front neck to hug the shoulder.

DESIGN NOTE

Exotic fabrics and accessories are the key to the appeal of this dress. Jewelled straps on glittering fabric and a purely ornamental chain with beads will pick up and repeat the sparkle of understated jewellery.

Long dress with draped overskirt

This overskirt can be attached to any slim-line skirt or dress.

Model a strapless dress and taper the skirt drastically to the ankle. Leave the centre back seam open. Make the overskirt separately before joining it to the centre back underskirt seam above the walking split.

Work on the cowl principle, turning under a deep facing and allowing the folds to fall at the centre front. In small sizes a single width of fabric on the straight grain is enough.

The beauty of this overskirt is the absence of side seams which would break the flow of the folds. The gathers are supported in the single centre back seam which may be left exposed or covered by a sash.

Fabric cut on the cross requires seaming. A split is necessary for walking room in both the underskirt and the overskirt.

The upper edge of the overskirt falls independently of the underskirt and is governed by the shape of the body. The lower part of the overskirt floats over the underskirt hem.

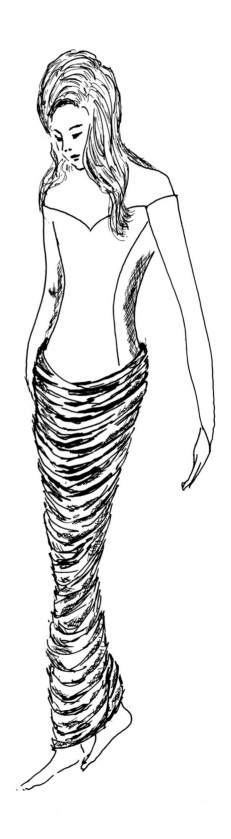

Fishtail dress

DESIGN NOTE

An elegant, classical style, the fishtail dress clings to the figure
to below the knee or calf, then cascades to simulate the tail of
a fish. More movement is possible if the front design line
begins at knee level. Many variations of this style are possible.
The 'tail' is very effective when fully gathered in fine net or
modelled in flounces.

Tape the design lines on the stand. Model the upper part of the
dress, and then follow the instructions for the fishtail skirt (p57).

Dress with ruched bodice and short full skirt

Use the principles learnt for the ruched bodice (p74) to make this dress. The straps are purely decorative, a vehicle for the diamonte which follows the panel lines at the front and back. Finish with a large back bow or trailing sashes over a short gathered skirt. Make the ruched sleeves separately. This dress is shown on the cover of the book.

90

Short evening dress cut on the cross

Most dress fabrics are 112-114cm (44-45")
wide. Cutting on the cross restricts the
possible dress length and most dresses are
seamed at the waistline or under the bust.
One solution is to gain 15cm (6") of fabric
by using separate shoulder straps. This
dress thus starts at the bust, ending just
below the knees.

This classic dress is modelled on the cross.
Allow the sides to hang straight or be
slightly flared, and the surplus fabric at the
upper edge to form a mini cowl effect.

Overskirt

A separate overskirt is a useful device for creating an alternative silhouette. An elegant sheath dress becomes a romantic ballgown when the overskirt is added.

Overskirts are usually wide at the hem, wrap around the waist, fasten at the centre front and fall open to reveal the dress beneath. The centre front may be shaped diagonally to reveal more of the lower dress. Overskirts are most effective when interlined with organdie or net and lined to cover seams.

Model over the dress that will be worn. The back of the overskirt may be lengthened to form a train.

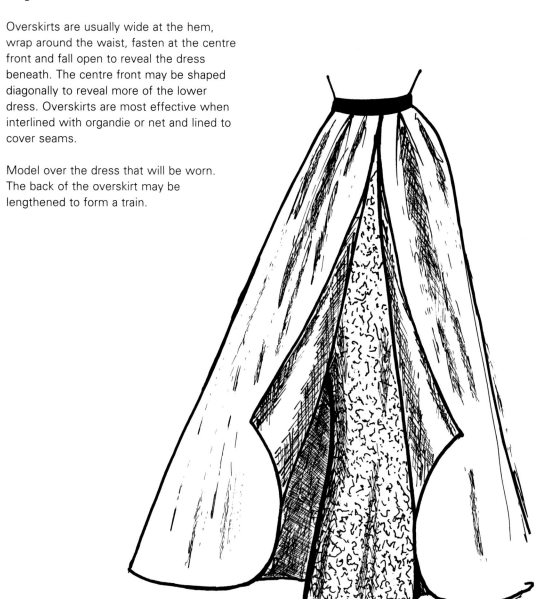

Shoulder drapes

Shoulder drapes can be an integral part of a dress or they can be detachable. They feature extensively in bridal and eveningwear, sometimes in a contrasting fabric.

Drapes look softer cut on the cross. Essential joins may be disguised as gathers or be covered with a decorative motif.

Most drapes fasten at the centre back. When circular and pulled over the head, they are not attached to the neckline near the opening.

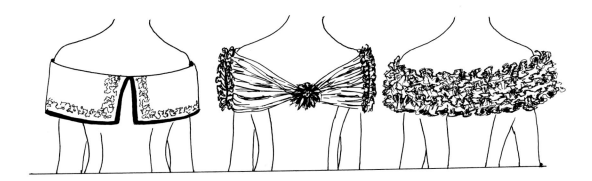

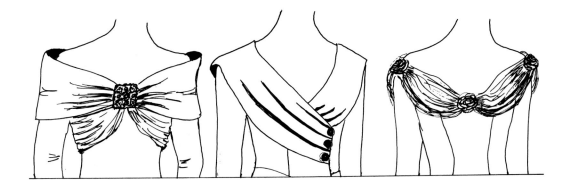

Glossary

anchor pin	pin used temporarily to control fabric
bias	any direction which is not the straight grain
boned foundation	boned bodice to support strapless garment
cross, on the cross	at an angle of 45° to the straight grain
lills	short pins used for taping the stand
nether garments	with a division for legs (eg shorts, trousers, swimwear)
ruching	gathered fabric enclosed between seams
straight grain	warp (lengthwise) and weft (crosswise) threads in fabric
strapless	garment not supported by the shoulders
stretch fabric	fabric with elastomeric fibre: extension (stretched); recovery (returned to original state)
toile	trial garment modelled and developed on a dress stand or person
tolerance (ease)	extra fabric to allow for body movement or to create a silhouette (designer ease)

Selected suppliers

DRESS STANDS

Kennett and Lindsell Ltd
Crow Lane
Romford
Essex RM7 OES

BOOKS AND SUPPLIES

R.D. Franks Ltd
Kent House
Market Place
London W1N 8EJ

Morplan
56 Great Titchfield Street
London W1P 8DX

FABRICS & HABERDASHERY

James Hare Silks
Monarch House
P.O. Box 72
Queen Street
Leeds LS1 1LX

John Lewis plc
Oxford Street
London W1A 1EX

Liberty plc
Regent Street
London
W1R 6AH

McCulloch & Wallis Ltd
25 Dering Street
London W1R 0BH

Whaleys (Bradford) Ltd
Harris Court Mills
Great Horton Road
Bradford
West Yorkshire BD7 4EQ

PATTERNMAKING BLOCKS
(SLOPERS)
COURSES & INFORMATION
BOOKLETS

Dawn Cloake
THE FASHION CONSULTANCY
P.O. Box 72
Hayes
Middlesex UB4 9YZ
UK
Tel/Fax: +44 (020) 8581 3390
www.fashionacademy.co.uk
www.designersfashionhub.co.uk
e-mail:
dawncloake@fashionacademy
                                .co.uk
and
dawn@cloake73.freeserve.co.uk

Further reading

Cloake, Dawn

Cutting and Draping Special Occasion Clothes,
B.T. Batsford Ltd, London, 1988

Lingerie Design on the Stand, **B.T. Batsford Ltd,
London, 2000**

Crawford, Connie Amaden

The Art of Fashion Draping, **Fairchild
Publications, New York, 1989**

Mee, Janice and Purdy, Michael

Modelling on the Dress Stand, **BSP Professional
Books, Oxford, 1987**

Silberberg, Lily and Shoben, Martin

The Art of Dress Modelling, **Butterworth
Heinemann, Oxford, 1992**

Stanley, Helen

Modelling and Flat Cutting for Fashion,
Hutchinson Education Ltd, 1983

Index